a + c black • london

coaching knowledges
understanding the dynamics of sport performance

jim denison

First published 2007 by
A & C Black Publishers Ltd
38 Soho Square, London W1D 3HB
www.acblack.com

ISBN-13: 978 0 7136 8186 4

A CIP catalogue record for this book is available from the British Library.

Note: It is always the responsibility of the individual to assess his or her own
fitness capability before participating in any training activity. Whilst every effort
has been made to ensure the content of this book is as technically accurate as
possible, neither the author nor the publishers can accept responsibility for any
injury or loss sustained as a result of the use of this material.

Text and cover design by James Watson
Cover photograph © istock.com

The publishers would like to thank TeamBath for permission to use the following
photographs: Lyn Gunson (p. 160); Chris Volley (p. 181) and Andy Tillson (p. 200).

This book is produced using paper that is made from wood grown in managed,
sustainable forests. It is natural, renewable and recyclable. The logging and manufac-
turing processes conform to the environmental regulations of the country of origin.

Typeset in Minion by Palimpsest Book Production Ltd, Grangemouth, Stirlingshire
Printed and bound in Norfolk

contents

preface v
acknowledgements vi

part 1 coaching today 1

chapter 1 **what is coaching?** 3
anthony bush

chapter 2 **coaching identity and
social exclusion** 24
eric anderson

chapter 3 **ethical coaching: gaining
respect in the field** 51
pirkko markula & montserrat martin

part 2 **coaching in practice** 83

chapter 4 **communicating with athletes** 85
imornefe bowes

chapter 5 **coaching experience,
coaching performance** 113
iain bates

chapter 6 **knowledge for sports coaching** . . . 138
zoe avner

part 3 **the coaching act** 159

chapter 7 **coach interview: lyn gunson** 160
leanne norman

chapter 8 **coach interview: chris volley** 181
jennifer hardes

chapter 9 **coach interview: andy tillson** 200
luke jones

list of contributors 216
index 218

preface

Every aspect of the 'coaching act', from conditioning and athlete development, to performance analysis and theories of training, is somehow influenced by the social construction of knowledge. A football team's tactics, for example, are shaped by the history of the game; a swim coach's workouts result from the conventions of scientific inquiry; and a basketball coach's relationship with his/ her athletes is always constrained by the limits of language.

However, when it comes to educating coaches, concerns over the social nature of coaching are often overlooked. Coaching's implicit social dynamics and human dimensions and the impact this has on every facet of the coaching act are rarely questioned and instead become subsumed beneath a false sense of objectivity and truth that pervades the sport sciences. This gap in understanding coaching as a human endeavour is this book's entry point. For what a coach does in training and on the sideline is far more complex and involved than setting exercises and drills and directing players into specific formations or positions.

In this book, we discuss and illustrate how the various knowledge domains that influence every coach's daily practice are constructed and informed by a range of social and cultural influences and knowledges. In this way, we hope to demonstrate that effective coaching concerns understanding the social nature of sport and viewing the coaching act as a dynamic, living process.

acknowledgements

I would like to thank Charlotte Croft from A&C Black whose idea it was to put this book together. Her support in the early stages of this project has always been appreciated. Also at A&C Black I would like to thank Lucy Beevor who has managed every aspect of the production process with efficiency and professionalism. Most importantly I would like to thank the contributors for their open mindedness and hard work in producing what I believe is an exciting collection of chapters that lays out an innovative and bold vision for coaching.

– Jim Denison

part 1
coaching today
bush, anderson, markula & martin

chapter 1
what is coaching?

anthony bush

introduction

In the profession of sports coaching there is an inexorable link between knowledge and competence. A designated level of competence and acquired knowledge is assumed if an individual obtains a 'coach education' related qualification. In research conducted by Pullo (1992) on strength and conditioning coaches, three of the characteristics in the profile of an 'effective' coach were formal coaching/sport related qualifications, including degree (and higher degree) level study. Jones (2005a) alludes to the recent recognition of coaching (i.e. improving the sporting performance of others) as a bone fide area of academic study, alongside the more established subject areas of sport psychology and physiology. The latest undergraduate and postgraduate admissions data for the UK indicates that, not only has coaching become established alongside the more traditional subject areas, it is eclipsing them in terms of provision at Higher Education (HE) institutions.

An undergraduate course search (UCAS, 2006a) reveals that, of the 1745 undergraduate (excluding foundation degree) sport courses, 192 concentrate on coaching (11%), while the closely-linked specialism of sport education accounts for 90 programmes (5.2%). The more established areas of sport psychology and sport/exercise physiology are the basis of 67 (3.8%) and 18 (1%) programmes respectively. It should be noted that the umbrella term 'sport science' (incorporating aspects of sociology, physiology, psychology and biomechanics) accounts for 1054 programmes (62.7%). It is also interesting to note that an undergraduate course search yields no hits for sport biomechanics, although searching for related specialist areas (e.g. 'Sports Performance Analysis') yields 11 programmes (0.6%).

Similar results are found when looking at postgraduate study in sport. The postgraduate course search (*The Guardian*, 2006) indicated that 49 institutions offered postgraduate qualifications in a sport-related field, of which 13 (26.5%) of the institutions offered coaching programmes, 10 (20.4%) sport/exercise physiology, eight (16.3%) sport/exercise psychology and only three (6.1%) sport biomechanics programmes. Coaching is not only flourishing as an academic subject at both undergraduate and postgraduate level, but is also emerging as a popular option in the more vocational HE qualifications (foundation degrees). Of the 198 foundation degrees in sport (including 'Sports Studies' and 'Sports Science'), 37 (18.7%) include 'coaching' in the programme title (UCAS, 2006b).

The expansion of coaching as an academic discipline is mirrored by its increased appearance in government policy. The prospect of hosting the Olympic and Paralympic Games in 2012 has provided a driving force for the recruitment and support of current and future coaches, which is seen as critical in ensuring a sporting legacy to reach beyond the 2012 Games (sports coach UK, 2006). Sports coach UK has been tasked with the development of the UK Coaching Framework in conjunction with national governing bodies of sport (NGBs) and the key funding agencies (UK Sport; the Department for Culture, Media and Sport; Home Country Sports Councils; the Department for Education and Skills; the British Olympic Association; Youth Sport Trust and SkillsActive). The UK Coaching Framework incorporates a range of initiatives, including a fast-track scheme for the production of 60 elite British coaches by 2012, the UK Coaching Certificate (UKCC) to endorse coach education programmes against agreed criteria, and the establishment of 3000 Community Sports Coaches (CSCs) and a network of 45 Coach Development Officers (CDOs). The Coaching Task Force report published in July 2002 resulted in the Government committing £28 million over a three-year period to coaching (DCMS, 2006a), and £60 million ring fenced between 2004 and 2008 to implement the UK Coaching Framework (DCMS, 2006b). The Government having also confirmed the allocation of £300 million to the athlete preparations for London 2012 (DCMS, 2006c), a significant investment is secured for coaching for the foreseeable future. This chapter attempts to demonstrate how the field of coaching has developed over the last two decades to gain such a prominent position within higher education and looks at what the future might hold for the development of coaching knowledge.

perspectives on coaching

Throughout the infancy of sports coaching research, debate surrounded the notion that coaching was essentially either a scientific or artistic activity, or even a blend of the two. The perception of coaching as a science implies that specific acquired knowledge can be prescribed in order to bring about incremental performance improvements. In comparison to coaching as a science, coaching as an art form results in performance improvement without rational, instrumental application of knowledge but through applying knowledge to a dynamic, complex environment in a less prescriptive, more creative and mystical manner. The perspective of coaching being a composite of science and art is supported by a number of coach educators (*see* Lyle, 1986; Potrac et al., 2000), although there are proponents for coaching being mainly scientific (*see* Balyi, 1992; Bompa, 1996; Bompa, 1999a; Bompa 1999b), or artistic (*see* Dick, 1989). Whichever perspective is adopted, there are important implications for the knowledge that underpins each. Woodman (1993) highlights the major areas of science that are impacting on coaching, 'anatomy, physiology, biochemistry, biomechanics, growth and development, statistics, tests and measurements, motor learning, psychology, sports medicine, nutrition, pedagogy, sociology, and information and communication technology' (pp. 1–2). The complex nature of the art of coaching, according to Woodman (1993, p. 4), emphasises the requirement for the coach to develop knowledge of an altogether different kind:

❛The coach, like the artist, must have creative flair and technical mastery over the material and tools used. In his [Dick, 1989] analogy the athlete is the instrument and the material, but, being an adaptive and reasoning being, is very complex to work with. Dick states that the coach must clearly understand the purpose of each practice and its relevance to the total scheme of preparation, while at the same time understand the growing, changing person of the athlete and the role of sport in his or her life.❜

Whether one predominantly supports a science or an art base to the profession, coaches must increase their knowledge in all aspects to be 'fully effective'. If we accept this holistic view of sports coaching and concede that a coach requires facets of both perspectives, then the debate *between* the two perspectives is now redundant:

⁶Lyle (1986) concludes that coaching is neither an art nor a science but a little of both. Lyle says that sports performance is not an exact science and that the individuality of the coach, decision-making based on experience, and the vagaries of the psychological aspects of performance point to human factors as a key part of the process. (Woodman, 1993, p. 5.)⁹

In reality, this is what we see 'on the ground', with coaches blending relevant components derived from both perspectives. In this book the authors examine the practice of coaching through investigating the range of knowledges necessary to coach effectively and holistic-ally. As the science/art debate subsided in the late 1980s, there was a need for a new characterisation of research perspectives on all areas of coaching.

Current scholarly activity can be seen to be underpinned by four approaches to sports coaching (Jones, 2005a). These are: psychological (*see* Bloom et al., 2003; Brewer & Jones, 2002; d'Arrippe-Longueville et al., 1998; Gilbert & Trudel, 2004), model-ling (*see* Côté et al., 1995; Cross & Lyle, 1999; Lyle, 2002; Sherman et al., 1997), sociological (*see* Cassidy et al., 2004; Jones, 2000; Jones et al., 2004; Jones et al., 2003; Lombardo, 1987; Potrac et al., 2002) and pedagogical (*see* Jones, 2005b; Jones & Wallace, 2005; Kidman, 2001; Potrac et al., 2000). It should be noted that these four approaches are not independent of each other; many of the authors who are identified as aligning with a particular approach might argue that to place their work in a particular category is an over-simplification, and that in a number of cases sports coaching research blurs the allocated boundaries. A presentation of the concepts central to each of the four approaches follows.

According to Jones (2005a), the parent discipline of coaching is psychology. Proponents of a psychological approach to coaching relate to the idea that 'it is all in the mind' and focus on areas such as decision making, skill acquisition, coach–athlete interactions, the role of the coach, self-esteem and cognition. Scholars working in this area see the development of sports coaching research as being parallel to the progress in psychological understanding. Historically, sports coaching was aligned with widely accepted and established behavioural and cognitive principles, before being enhanced by a branch of psychology that added the human dimension, namely humanistic psychology. This 1950s' development within psychology has remained a domineering influence over contemporary sports coaching research. This was demonstrated by Lyle (2002) embracing the humanistic approach as a 'benchmark' for behaviour in sports coaching. Recent developments in the field of psychology continue to inform contemporary sports coaching research, which has largely remained faithful to the psychological approach.

The modelling approach to coaching is based on the premise that 'coach effectiveness' or 'coaching success' can be achieved through the identification, analysis and control of variables that affect athlete performance, and the application of a sequential process. This sequential view of coaching conveniently allows for modification of the process to achieve success. The modelling perspective is highlighted by Kidman & Hanrahan (2004), 'if coaches are not achieving success (however it is defined), they need to look at changing what they are doing, that is, changing the process' (p. 16). Jones (2005a) describes the existence of two forms of research within this approach to sports coaching, 'models of' the coaching process that are based on empirical research investigating effective coaching practice, and 'models for' the coaching process as idealistic representations that develop from the identification of a set of assumptions about the process.

The precursor to a sociological approach to coaching according to Jones (2005a), was a perceived dissatisfaction with the presentation of coaching as a sequential process, which was felt to be an oversimplification of a much more complex procedure. Jones et al. (2004) indicate that 'a professional coach is much more than a subject matter specialist and a systematic method applier' (p. 2). The sociological approach is concerned with looking at issues largely ignored by the psychological and modelling approaches to sports coaching, often the elements defined as 'intuition', 'wisdom', or the 'art of coaching'. Key issues dealt with under the sociological approach are the acquisition; maintenance and advancement of social power; the constructionist nature of coaching knowledge; the social role of the coach; coaches' philosophies; coaches' agency; coaches' interactions; the coaching environment and the pedagogic setting. In essence, scholarly activity within this approach aims to question the practices presented in other research perspectives (and often taken for granted) that portray an 'oddly inhuman account of this most human of jobs' (Connell, 1985, p. 4).

A pedagogical approach to sports coaching encroaches into the territory of the sociological approach in the area of the learning [coaching] environment, referred to in this context as the 'pedagogic setting'. The pedagogic approach is based on the premise that coaching is fundamentally a teaching activity, with the goal being athlete learning. In addition to the identifiable links to the sociological approach, the roots of the scholarly activity defined as a pedagogical approach to sports coaching are also linked to sports coaching's parent discipline, psychology. The behaviourist nature of the pedagogic approach to sports coaching defines the topics that are open to investigation; they must be observable and measurable. Deviation from the psychological approach to sports coaching occurs as the development of an individual's cognitive and meta-cognitive strategies, and other internal processes, are not considered. Jones (2005a) suggests that this approach to sports coaching has provided useful information, but its one-dimensional view cannot be generalised across contexts. Despite its limitations, there has been an emergence of recent scholarly activity that has used educational theory to reconceptualise sports coaching as a critical pedagogical process (*see* Jones, 2005b; Jones & Wallace, 2005).

Authors would concede that a blurring of the boundaries between the four approaches to sports coaching does exist, opening up the possibility of scholarly activity being increasingly reflective of the more complex nature of coaching. For example, drawing on ideas from social psychology and using a combination of the assumptions made in both the sociological and psychological approaches to sports coaching, Bowes & Jones (2006) used relational schemas and complexity theory to put forward an alternative theoretical framework for a more realistic conception of coaching. What Bowes & Jones seek to do is to familiarise coaches and coach educators with the reality that coaching is in essence a complex, interactive process, and that the understanding of different concepts of coaching will ultimately make coaches better prepared to cope with the demands placed upon them. In emphasising the need for coach education to take a fuller account of the interactive, social nature of coaching, Bowes & Jones (2006) demonstrate the importance of moving beyond more traditional coach education models towards a presentation of coaching as a dynamic process that takes place within the social arena and not in isolation.

the contribution of this book to coaching knowledge

To move scholarly activity forward in the field of sports coaching, researchers will need to embrace the challenge brought to existing research approaches by new perspectives that have emerged on the basis of different sets of assumptions. There is a need to expand the research approaches from the existing parameters offered by the four research approaches (psychological; modelling; pedagogical and sociological) to 'blended' approaches, such as those offered by Bowes & Jones' (2006) use of social psychology, and approaches that view coaching holistically, reflecting both the social nature of sport as well as the dynamic process that is the act of coaching. Therefore, the aim of this book is to present approaches to sports coaching to the reader that are not constrained by existing boundaries to investigation, that illustrate how the various areas of knowledge that influence every coach's daily practice are delivered, constructed and informed by a range of environmental, social and cultural influences.

I will first offer an overview of the book's structure to give the reader a feel for the direction of the text, before offering a commentary on the content of the chapters. This is intended to reflect three distinctive collections (sections) of papers. In 'Part 1: coaching today', the emphasis is to provide the reader with a wider 'lens' with which to view sports coaching research and then to reinforce this new 'receptiveness' by unpicking the key coaching concepts of identity, relationships and knowledges. The second section, 'Part 2: coaching in practice', is a collection of contributions from practitioners, where important concepts such as communicating with athletes and the impact of coaches' experience are investigated. The third section, 'Part 3: the coaching act', presents the reality of coaching in practice, with particular focus on the concepts discussed in the book, reinforcing the book's relevance for scholars and practitioners of sports coaching research.

This introductory chapter is followed by a chapter from Eric Anderson ('Coaching identity and social exclusion') in which he challenges the myth that sport is socio-positive and inclusive, responsible for building self-esteem, developing teamwork and improving the health of individuals and the community as a whole. It is a socio-negative perspective to sport presented by Anderson that will challenge many of the assumptions that scholars, athletes and coaches hold about the position and role of sport in society. Anderson specifically focuses on how coaches shape their coaching identity and how they use their agency through socialisation to the coaching profession to reproduce sport as a socially exclusive territory. The mechanisms that produce sport's social outcomes are investigated followed by a discussion of the powerful socio-negative outcomes of these mechanisms: misogyny, homophobia, ableism, racism and violence. Anderson then shows how coaches have been socialised into the social exclusion model, and, more importantly, proceeds to offer practical examples of how a coach might best use their agency to move sport into a more inclusive direction. Enhancing 'inclusivity' in sport, although ignored in current sports coaching literature, must be seen as a central tenet of future coach educa- tion programmes so that the next generation of coaches develop an awareness of the power and influence of their agency.

Pirkko Markula and Monserrat Martin's chapter ('Ethical coaching: gaining respect in the field') is framed within the context that the coach-athlete relationship cannot be viewed in isolation from the surrounding network of which both the athlete and coach belong. In this chapter, one specific aspect of the coach- athlete relationship is examined – respect – as shaped by social and cultural forces that surround the coach. To present 'respect' in the coach–athlete relationship, they use a strong influence from both the sociological and pedagogical approaches to sports coaching. Respect in contemporary coaching literature is a much- ignored aspect of the act of coaching, and what Markula and Martin attempt to do is discuss the coach–athlete relationship as a power relationship in order to explain what this might mean in terms of gaining respect and being a 'credible' coach. They then indi- cate that due to the nature of power relations it is important that coaches use their knowledge in an effective way, that they actively question the knowledge they possess, and use it ethically to main- tain the respect of their athletes. The authors use compelling examples to illustrate situations where a coach faces a need for respect from their players. The chapter concludes by reflecting on the situations that might confront coaches as a result of the relationships between their athletes, the athletes' parents or the national and international level administration of their sport. Markula and Martin highlight the need to establish what constitutes ethical coaching behaviour, and for coaches to define their ethical goals and to articulate them clearly to their athletes. This places an emphasis on a shared understanding between coach and athlete of their reasons for being involved in sport.

The second section of the book ('Part 2: coaching in practice') commences with a chapter by Imornefe Bowes ('Communicating with athletes') in which Bowes once again challenges the assumptions made in sports coaching literature. He indicates that coaching texts describe a straightforward account of steps to follow when coaches communicate with athletes and that this simplified account of coach–athlete interaction is far from the reality of coaching practice. Bowes' main contention is that communication is about developing a shared meaning between coach and athlete, and that it is this *construction* of knowledge that takes place as a result of the interaction that leads to the creation of new collective knowledge between coach and athlete. Bowes outlines the widely accepted and typically unchallenged account of communication within sports coaching texts, before applying schema theory from the field of cognitive psychology to situate the coach and athlete as 'constructive thinkers'. To allow practitioners to implement some of the concepts discussed in the chapter, Bowes concludes by identifying strategies that, when utilised in a coaching context, would facilitate the development of a shared meaning between coach and athlete.

Iain Bates' chapter ('Coaching experience, coaching performance') is framed within an acceptance that the act of coaching is complex and constructed around social experiences and exposure to the working context. The emphasis of the chapter is that experience plays a pivotal role in the development of a coach's knowledge, and that reflective practice can be employed by practitioners to enhance their coaching performance (or *effectiveness*) through the generation of a dynamic and constantly evolving knowledge base. This dynamic knowledge base facilitates coach effectiveness through coaches becoming more secure in their coaching environment. Bates presents two examples of 'reflection in practice' to demonstrate how this process can be implemented into a coach's routine as a core competency of practice. Central to coaches adopting this process, Bates argues that, because of the current limitations of coach education programmes (i.e. struggling to integrate the concept of ambiguity and the changing social dynamic that typifies the coaching environment), coaches must be the ones to take responsibility for their own continuing professional development.

Continuing with the ideas of communication, complexity and reflection, Zoe Avner in her chapter ('Knowledge for sports coaching') provides a personal account of her experiences as a football player in France. Avner adopts a critical perspective to comment on power and knowledge in coaching and how these can easily be abused by the uninformed coach with potentially harmful consequences for the athlete. In this way her chapter is about how coaching must always be done with the understanding of the complexities of individual and cultural relationships.

The third section of the book ('Part 3: the coaching act') uses in-depth interviews with three master coaches from the University of Bath to show how each coach applies a breadth of knowledge to manage the complex dynamics of high performance sport. The importance of these three chapters is heightened by the fact that both male and female coaches are represented, as are coaches from both team and individual sports, and also coaches with differing degrees of experience within the profession.

The first interview with Lyn Gunson (netball), conducted by Leanne Norman, is grounded in a feminist cultural studies conceptual framework and endeavours to illuminate the complexities facing women in elite coaching positions. In addition to this the questioning reveals how women leaders are received in a male dominated profession and also how women coaches have negotiated various social expectations and cultural norms to reach their position. Norman takes the reader on an insightful journey of Gunson's professional development; influential role models (or lack of them in a coaching context); body image difficulties facing female athletes; personal values; the roles and routine of a professional coach; the autocratic nature of male coaches; the adaptation of coaching styles and the impact this has on athletes; accountability of a professional coach; the power of administrators; men coaching netball; and the conflict of being a woman and a sportswoman.

The second interview with Chris Volley (triathlon) is conducted by Jennifer Hardes and offers a view of a professional coach at the start of his career. A notable distinction between Volley and Gunson is that Volley works with both a performance group of athletes as well as the student triathlon club. Volley's interview portrays the benefits of working from a 'blank canvas' as a new coach in an institution; making the move from athlete to coach; the dynamics of the transition from 'my friend' to 'my coach'; developing relationships and trust with the athletes; the balancing act of athlete empowerment versus athlete control; personal values; coaching a range of abilities; using multidisciplinary institutional expertise; the evolution of an adaptive coaching philosophy; and the intuitive nature of coaching. Volley further articulates his beliefs on the social construction of a sports coach's knowledge; the nuances of working with athletes from an individual sport in a group setting; the approaches to coaching male and female athletes; reflections on the overuse of praise with his athletes; and athletes and coaches learning from the mistakes that they make.

The third interview with Andy Tillson (football), who spoke to Luke Jones, gives us a different perspective again on the profession of coaching. Tillson reached the heights of captaining a professional football side in the Football League (Bristol Rovers), before making the transition to semi-professional football in combination with a career away from sport, before embarking on a professional coaching career. Tillson articulates this transition from professional sport and his desire to get into coaching, while highlighting the therapeutic effect that coaching can give an elite athlete in coping with the transition from 'player' to 'non-player'. Tillson expresses the influence that captaincy, mentors and role models has had on his ability to become a professional coach. Tillson describes how his approach to coaching has been shaped by his experience and how his current practice is evolving on the basis of continual reflection on his coaching performance. He suggests how the culture of the football environment leads to the reproduction of coaching habits by ex-professional footballers, and highlights the importance of this stage of his coaching career in developing into a more effective coach. The importance of relationships and respect; the development of individual players within the context of the team performance; player responsibility; differences between coaching and managing, and the coach's role in motivating their athletes are also considered.

conclusion

This introductory chapter has depicted the rise of sports coaching as a bone fide area of sport-related study and also its emergence as a central tenet within government sport policy for the fore-seeable future. In light of these 'recent' developments a greater emphasis is therefore placed on the professionalisation of sports coaching, and concurrently on scholarly activity in sports coaching to inform coaches through vocational (professional) and academic coach education programmes. This chapter has documented the historical development of scholarly activity in sports coaching, from its inception as a scientific or artistic activity, through its classifications as being essentially psychological, modelling, sociological or pedagogical in its approach, towards a new holistic characterisation of sports coaching. The emphasis of the book, therefore, is to challenge the assumptions presented in current sports coaching literature, to remove the barriers of previous scholarly activity, and to present the reality of the act of coaching as a complex, dynamic, social process.

references

Balyi, I. (1992). 'Beyond Barcelona: A contemporary critique of the theory of periodisation'. In *Beyond Barcelona*. 4th Elite Coaches Seminar. Canberra; Australian Coaching Council.

Bloom, G., Stevens, D. and Wickwire, T. (2003). 'Expert coaches' perceptions of team building'. *Journal of Applied Sport Psychology*. 15 (2), pp. 129–143.

Bompa, T.O. (1999a). *Periodisation Training for Sport*. Champaign, IL; Human Kinetics.

Bompa, T.O. (1999b). *Periodisation: Theory and Methodology of Training* (4th edition). Champaign, IL; Human Kinetics.

Bompa, T.O. (1996). *Periodisation of Strength*. Toronto; Veritas.

Bowes, I. & Jones, R.L. (2006). 'Working at the edge of chaos: Understanding coaching as a complex, interpersonal system'. *The Sport Psychologist*, 20, pp. 235–245.

Brewer, C.J. & Jones, R.L. (2002). 'A five-stage process for establishing contextually valid systematic observation instruments: The case of rugby union'. *The Sport Psychologist*, 16 (2), pp. 139–161.

Cassidy, T., Jones, R.L. & Potrac, P. (2004). *Understanding Sports Coaching: The Social, Cultural and Pedagogical Foundations of Coaching Practice*. London; Routledge.

Connell, R. (1985). *Teachers' Work*. London; Allen & Unwin.

Côté, J., Sammela, J., Trudel, P., Baria, A. & Russell, S. (1995). 'The coaching model: A grounded assessment of expert gymnastic coaches knowledge'. *Journal of Sport and Exercise Psychology*, 17 (1), pp. 1–17.

Cross, N. & Lyle, J. (1999). *The Coaching Process: Principles and Practice for Sport*. Oxford; Butterworth-Heinemann.

d'Arrippe-Longueville, F., Fournier, J.F. & Dubois, A. (1998). 'The perceived effectiveness of interactions between expert French judo coaches and elite female athletes'. *The Sport Psychologist*, 12, pp. 317–332.

DCMS (2006a). 'Sport: Coaching'. Retrieved 19 April 2006 from www.culture.gov.uk/sport/coaching.htm

DCMS (2006b). 'Sport: Coaching'. Retrieved 24 July 2006 from www.culture.gov.uk/sport/coaching.htm

DCMS (2006c). UK Sport press release. Retrieved 19 April 2006 from www.culture.gov.uk/global/press_notices/archive_2006/dcms_uksport.htm

Dick, F.W. (1989). *Sports Training Principles* (2nd edition). London; A&C Black.

Gilbert, W. & Trudel, P. (2004). 'The role of the coach: How model youth team sport coaches frame their roles'. *The Sport Psychologist*, 18, pp. 21–43.

The Guardian (2006). Postgraduate course search. Retrieved 20 April 20 2006 from http://guardian.uk.studylink.com/index.html

Jones, R.L. (2005a). 'Higher education academy network for hospitality, leisure, sport and tourism: Resource guide to sports coaching'. Retrieved 10 April 2006 from www.hlst.heacademy.ac.uk/Resources/coaching.pdf

Jones, R.L. (ed.) (2005b). *The Sports Coach as Educator: Reconceptualising Sports Coaching*. London; Routledge.

Jones, R.L. (2000). 'Toward a sociology of coaching'. In *Sociology of Sport: Theory and Practice*. Jones, R.L. & Armour, K.M. (eds.) (2000). London; Pearson.

Jones, R.L. & Wallace, M. (2005). 'Another bad day at the training ground: Coping with ambiguity in the coaching context'. *Sport, Education and Society*, 10 (1), pp. 119–134.

Jones, R.L., Armour, K.M. & Potrac, P. (2004). *Sports Coaching Cultures: From Practice to Theory*. London; Routledge.

Jones, R.L., Armour, K.M. & Potrac, P. (2003). 'Constructing expert knowledge: A case study of a top-level professional soccer coach'. *Sport, Education and Society*, 8 (2), pp. 213–229.

Kidman, L. (ed.). (2001). *Innovative Coaching: Empowering Your Athletes*. Christchurch, NZ; Innovative Communications.

Kidman, L. & Hanrahan, S. (2004). *The Coaching Process: A Practical Guide to Improving Your Effectiveness* (2nd edition). Palmerston North; Dunmore.

Lombardo, B.J. (1987). *The Humanistic Coach: From Theory to Practice*. Springfield; Ill; C.C. Thomas.

Lyle, J. (2002). *Sports Coaching Concepts: A Framework for Coaches' Behaviour*. London; Routledge.

Lyle, J. (1986). 'Coach education: Preparation for a profession'. In *Proceedings of the 8th Commonwealth and International Conference on Sport, Physical Education, Dance, Recreation and Health*. London; E. & F.N. Spon.

Potrac, P., Jones, R.L. & Armour, K.M. (2002). '"It's all about getting respect": The coaching behaviours of an expert English soccer coach'. *Sport, Education and Society*, 7 (2), pp. 183–202.

Potrac, P., Brewer, C., Jones, R.L., Armour, K. & Hoff, J. (2000). 'Toward an holistic understanding of the coaching process'. *Quest*, 52, pp. 186–199.

Pullo, F.M. (1992). 'A profile of NCAA division 1 strength and conditioning coaches'. *Journal of Applied Sport Science Research*, 6 (1), pp. 55–62.

Sherman, C., Crassini, B., Maschette, W. & Sands, R. (1997). 'Instructional sport psychology: A reconceptualisation of sports coaching as sports instruction'. *International Journal of Sport Psychology*, 28 (2), pp. 103–125.

sports coach UK (2006). 'UK action plan for coaching'. Retrieved 20 April 2006 from www.sportscoachuk.org/About+Us/UKAPC/introduction.htm

UCAS (2006a). Universities and Colleges Admissions Service course search: sport. Retrieved April 20 2006 from http://search.ucas.co.uk/cgi-bin/hsrun/search/search/StateId/R1L76oGOsaKBGEOItizM_0NeCk5NA-4SzG/HAHTpage/search.HsKeywordSearch.whereNext?query=677&word=SPORT

UCAS (2006b). Universities and Colleges Admissions Service course search: foundation degree. Retrieved 20 April 2006 from http://develop.ucas.com/cgi-bin/hsrun.exe/General/FDCourseSearch/FDCourseSearch.hjx;start=FDCourseSearch.HsForm.run

Woodman, L. (1993). 'Coaching: A science, an art, an emerging profession'. *Sport Science Review*, 2 (2), pp. 1–13.

chapter 2
coaching identity and social exclusion

eric anderson

introduction

There is a persistent myth – a near-hegemonic belief – concerning sport and society. It is a myth that purports sport to be a socio-positive, inclusive and egalitarian meritocracy. The cultural strength of this myth is so strong that parents, players, coaches, scholars and fans tend to overlook the large number of problems associated with the culture of sport and the way we structure and run it. When the utility of sport and its ability to produce socio-positive outcomes is examined, there is often a negation of the socio-negative aspects through a 'it does more good than harm' framework. Yet, there is no 'first do no harm' creed in sport. Rather, the mantra is generally 'win at all costs' despite the breadth and intensity of those costs. Thus, few people intricately involved with sport question whether sport – or at least the way we play and value it – is worth the toll on our bodies, minds and society.

Paradoxically, social thinking on sport commonly regards most sporting activity as a vessel for the building of self-esteem, the teaching of teamwork and for delivering improved health to the individual and community, despite this paradigm's failure to prove this under empirical scrutiny. Miracle & Reese (1994), for example, show that only a few children seem to have their self-esteem raised in sport, and those who do largely do so at the expense of others. Similarly, rather than sport teaching children to work together, it more often pits them against one another for social promotion, creating social division instead of cohesion. Finally, the health benefits attributed to most sport may easily be maintained by a walking or jogging programme, which generally incurs less risk of injury, social marginalisation or potentiality of being subject to a coach's physical and verbal abuse.

Specific to the focus of this chapter, however, sport and those who coach it have traditionally, although often unknowingly, promoted misogyny, racism, homophobia, violence and ability-status discrimination. This is particularly true among boys and men, but also applies to girls and women. Thus, rather than sport benefiting the whole of a society, I maintain that organised team sport largely serves a limited number of athletically talented, able-bodied, white, heterosexual males.

In this chapter I focus on just one aspect of the complicated social milieu that helps sport reproduce itself as a socially exclusionary terrain. Namely, I illustrate how individual coaches are conditioned to shape their coaching identity and are influenced to utilise their agency to maintain, instead of challenge, the status quo. Thus, in explaining the socialisation process of coaches into their profession, I illustrate the structural and cultural influences that frequently direct them to utilise their agency for the reproduction of sport as a socially exclusive territory.

To begin, I highlight how sport structures and cultures operate. Next, I describe how these influence sport's socio-negative outcomes, listing the specifics of discrimination against various groups of people. I then move onto a discussion of the role coaches play in this: how they are socialised and what they can do to make sport more inclusive.

the mechanisms that produce sport's social outcomes

Before we can understand the role of the coach in reproducing inequality, we must first understand the system of socialisation from which coaches emerge. The development of coaches who reproduce sport as a socially exclusive environment is influenced by a number of variables, but the most salient are the social structure of sport and the culture of sport.

The *social structure* of sport refers to the manner in which the game is physically structured and played; the manner in which athletes are promoted, divided and rewarded. For example, one structure (of almost all sport) is that it is played to determine a sole winning individual or team over other losing individuals or teams. Yet, this is not the only structure upon which sport can be played. One could, for example, follow the historical tradition of many Native American tribes and begin a sporting competition with two teams of unequal ability (Oxendine, 1988) adding or removing players until all teams achieve equal parity.

This is the way children naturally play games; that is to say before adults socialise them into what they maintain to be 'fair' rules from an adult perspective. Yet, before adult socialisation into sport, children tend to balance teams out to equal ability, even if it means one side has considerably more players than the other. Children seem to believe that equal ability is what is 'fair,' not equal team size. Also, they seem to feel that a close competition is what is fun and fair about sport, and they create structures to assure this. Thus children of lesser ability might be given more tries or allowed a greater margin for error. Alternatively, a sporting game could be played without keeping score at all. Sport can be enjoyed for the sake of movement alone. Competition is not necessary to enjoy sport.

A final example of the influence of structure on sport comes from the near total segregation that occurs in sport. Sport is unique in that it nearly always segregates women from men – something more akin to orthodox religions than state-sponsored social welfare programmes.

The *culture of sport* simply refers to the values and norms associated with any given sport. The collective value of all sports can also be generalised into that of a sporting ethos for our society as a whole. You have heard the mantras before; sport is supposed to teach the value of 'hard work' and sport certainly values 'giving it one's all'. But there are other creeds within our sporting culture. We value a hyper-masculine disposition in sport. There is after all 'no crying in baseball', there is no room 'for a sore loser', and 'there is no "I" in team'. Dropping out of sport is frowned upon, as is 'throwing like a girl', challenging a coach's intelligence or authority or giving less than one hundred per cent.

Finally, and of primary concern to this chapter, the socially exclusive nature of sport is influenced by coaches who progressed through this system, and may therefore utilise their individual agency to reproduce a faulty system they believe worked for them. But the coach maintains a great deal of power in socialising individuals into a different belief system and, to a lesser extent, the coach also maintains the ability to alter certain sport structures too. Thus, as gatekeepers, coaches maintain a great deal of sway in determining the social outcomes of sport.

There are several reasons why coaches maintain such power in shaping the norms of their teams. First, social psychologists frequently refer to five basic types of power (French & Raven, 1959), of which coaches often possess all five. And while it is not absolutely necessary to understand exactly what and how each of these powers is and operates, it is important to understand that few other occupations/professions offer individuals the ability to associate with all five types of power (Jones, Armour & Potrac, 2004). These powers are described as:

1 *Legitimate*, defined as power given by one's elected or appointed status.
2 *Coercive*, defined as power because of one's ability to take something away.
3 *Reward*, defined as power derived from the ability to give something desired.
4 *Expert*, defined as power accorded individuals who have undergone formal training.
5 *Referent*, defined as power given because of the respect the coach might have as an inspiration or mentor.

Clearly coaches use reward power by offering players social promotions, more playing time or public praise, and they use coercive power in punishing athletes with the opposite. Coaches establish their legitimacy in the eyes of their athletes primarily through having 'come up' through the system, often as a successful player first and then by producing quality athletes. This legitimacy, coupled with the title 'coach,' is then thought (often erroneously) to make one an expert, as coaches are assumed to possess the technical knowledge beneficial to promote performance. Finally, coaches sometimes gain the respect of their athletes through referent power because athletes desire to accomplish the same feats, times or levels of play, or because they look to the coach as a mentor or parental figure.

the socio-negative outcomes of these mechanisms

sport and misogyny

The reproduction of anti-feminine attitudes among men in sport is achieved by both structural and cultural methods. First, few other institutions naturalise the structural segregation of men and women nearly so perfectly as team sports (Messner, 2002). While occupational sex segregation is declining in other institutions (Cotter, et. al., 1995; Johnson, 1998; Rotolo & Wharton, 2004), institutionalised, competitive team sports remain segregated through formal and social reasoning (Messner, 2002). This segregation has many historical sources including the belief that women were not physically or emotionally capable of playing sport and the overriding belief that women were not naturally inclined to participate in such activity (Crosset, 1990; Hargreaves, 1993; Kidd, 1990; Whitson, 1990). Although women have made many gains in playing team sport in the past several decades, as the number of women who play sport increases, the proportion of women who coach has decreased (Stangl & Kane, 1991).

And while we may no longer believe that sporting participation is physically incompatible with womanhood, a still salient cultural variable in men's sports is that masculinity remains predicated in not associating with femininity (Anderson, 2005). The reasons for this are multiple and complex, but the equation of predicating masculinity in opposition to femininity is one of sociology's most durable findings (Kimmel, 1994). Accordingly, the social world created around men's team sports is one of subversion for the respect of women, who are not viewed as worthy participants in the sporting terrain. Instead of valuing the athleticism of women, their social location in relationship to men is one that frequently places them as bodies to be pursued and conquered by the 'rightful' participants of the sporting terrain. It has even been argued that it leads to elevated rates of sexual violence against women by participants of certain team sports (Crosset, 1990, 2000; Crosset, Benedict & MacDonald, 1995).

sport and homophobia

While there are few structural mechanisms keeping gay and lesbian athletes from equal sporting participation, there are extra-ordinarily strong cultural determinants: indeed, sport has been described as one of the last bastions of institutionalised homo-phobia (Anderson, 2005). This is evidenced by the near-total absence of openly gay or lesbian athletes in the professional, collegiate, and lower ranks of sporting systems. This, however, does not mean that gay and lesbian athletes avoid sport alto-gether. Rather, it suggests that they are simply too afraid to come out (in any real numbers) in what they perceive to be a socially hostile environment.

Yet it should not be a surprise to learn that closeted or selectively closeted gay and lesbian athletes do exist (at even the highest levels of sport). This is because nearly all kids (regardless of their sexual orientation) are socialised into sport through networks of friends and through compulsory participation in physical education. Furthermore, although it may seem that gay men might be repelled by the homophobia within sport, research suggests that many are drawn to sport precisely because they seek the masculinising and heterosexualising veneer it provides (Anderson, 2005).

sport and ableism

Disabled people face both structural and cultural obstacles to equal sporting participation. Perhaps the structural conditions of many organised sporting practices are the most salient obstacle to full-inclusion. Many sports simply remain inaccessible to people with various types of disabilities. Consequently, adaptations to these sports (such as wheelchair basketball) have helped promote athletic participation among the disabled, but such advances are often subject to class discrimination. A running prosthetic for below-the-knee amputees costs about £7,613 (US $15,000), and a light-framed runner who uses it to put in just 40 miles (64km) a week needs to replace it once a year.

But there is also a degree of cultural influence over the barriers to equal athletic participation among disabled people. Much of the focus on disabilities seems to remain on what people can't do, rather than what they can. It was for these purposes that, in 1989, the International Paralympics Committee (IPC) was organised to mobilise a number of individual organisations and heighten the public profile of disabled athletes. Yet the IPC remains extraordinarily exclusive as to what type of athletes, from what sports, and of what events are included in the Paralympics. Rather than adopting a gay games model of total inclusivity and encouraging the development of a community of Paralympic athletes, the games have modelled themselves after the hyper-competitive and exclusive nature of the Olympics. Thus, the Paralympics severely restricts the number of athletes that may participate, leaving only the elite to play.

While separate sporting leagues and organisations have helped promote athleticism among the disabled, much of this participation remains segregated from mainstream sport, and few coaches are trained to understand the special needs of athletes with disabilities. So, rather than the rules of basketball changing to adapt disabled athletes who might want to adapt play in a given school or community league, disabled athletes are instead segregated from 'able-bodied' athletes.

sport and racism

Although there are many racial and ethnic minorities, black athletes are examined as the example in this chapter because they have taken a long and difficult road to gain what little space they maintain in sport. African Americans have been particularly oppressed in the United States, where they have had to struggle against centuries of slavery and another century of legalised segregation. Remarkably, some observers maintain that sport is no longer racist. These critically ill-informed thinkers show that in American sport, black athletes are well represented in basketball, football and, to a lesser extent, baseball. However, it is important to note that black athletes, in any real numbers, are limited to just these three sports. Coakley (1998) says:

> Since the 1950s, the sport participation of blacks has been concentrated in just a handful of sports. Even in the 1990s, the 34 million African Americans are underrepresented or non-existent in most sports at most levels of competition . . . there is a virtual absence of black athletes in archery, auto-racing, badminton, bowling, canoeing/kayaking, cycling, diving, equestrian events, field hockey, figure skating, golf, gymnastics, hockey, motocross, rodeo, rowing, sailing, shooting, alpine and Nordic skiing, soccer, softball, swimming, table tennis, team handball, tennis, volleyball, water polo, yachting, and many field events in track and field.

Also, when blacks athletes are represented in sport they tend to come from positions that are less central to the outcome of the game. Thus, in baseball they are much more likely to play a field position than pitcher, and in American football they are much more likely to be a wide-receiver than a quarterback.

sport and violence

The violent nature of sport (particularly as one matriculates up the sporting hierarchy) promotes the social exclusion of many types of people. First, the physical violence that is intended or un-intended in sport prohibits those without enough muscle mass from effectively participating. More significantly, the violence associated with playing through pain, taking risks and giving it all means that a large number of athletes are excluded from participation due to injury. Finally, the intra-personal violence associated with fighting and intimidation influences some parents (perhaps rightfully) to withhold their children from these types of sport, preventing many individuals from voluntarily playing them.

Much of the violence (against self and others) found in sport can be attributed to the structure of sport. This is particularly made clear in contact sports. But much of the violence in sport also comes from the way we play it, requiring a winner, which necessitates success being achieved only by another's loss. In this manner, Lester Thurow (1985) describes sport as being a zero-sum game. Sport is a social situation in which one person's success must come at the expense of others. Exemplifying this, coaches and athletes frequently express ill feelings toward their competitor as they have been socialised into an in-group/out-group perspective that is predicated upon establishing the other team as the enemy. Rather than viewing competitors as agents in co-operation to bring out one's best, others (often even members from the same team) are viewed as obstacles in the path of obtaining cultural and economic power. 'In order for me to win, you must lose.' Violence (conscious or not, intentional or unintentional) becomes an acceptable tool for achieving this victory. Hence, the structure of the sport produces the culture of the sport.

a coach's role in social exclusion

As gatekeepers to sport, coaches play a vital role in the reproduction of this socially exclusive terrain. Individual coaches utilise their agency (willingly or not) to help reproduce sport as a socially exclusive institution, or to challenge these tenets and help open sport to inclusivity. How coaches use their agency in shaping sport to be inclusive or exclusive of gay men and women and/or feminine-acting heterosexual men is in some ways obvious. For example, the use of homophobic, femphobic and misogynistic language clearly creates a culture of hate that discourages many people from coming out to play, or coming out while playing. But how coaches use their agency to promote ableism, racism and violence is a bit less obvious.

ableism

Because the structure of most sport places most types of athlete with a disability (or a lesser ability) at a disadvantage and, because the culture of sport influences coaches to overly value winning (the measure by which most judge a coach's success), athletes with disabilities are often thought to be undesirable for a team's 'success'. This has two meanings for the social exclusion of disabled athletes in sport. First, coaches are less likely to intentionally seek out disabled athletes for participation on their teams. Drawing upon my own experience as a high school distance running coach, the common practice for coaches to identify and recruit potential team members was to ask the PE teacher to get their students to run a mile. The coach would then talk to the fastest finishers of that mile and attempt to recruit them to his/her sport. It is not likely, however, that a disabled runner will be placed at the top of this event and they are therefore overlooked.

More insidious, able-bodied coaches concerned with their win-loss record are more likely to reject disabled athletes outright than coaches who are concerned with the quality of character they develop among their charges. Again, drawing upon my experience is the case of CJ, who was a top-notch college runner at the University of California Irvine. He was diagnosed with bone cancer – necessitating the removal of a foot. After chemotherapy and amputation C.J. wanted to return to his team, but his coach denied him. Sadly, this is not the only time I have heard of such a story. Highlighting the opportunity his coach missed, as a lecturer at the same university I learned of C.J.'s situation and volunteered to coach him: within a year he broke three world records for his division of distance running.

racism

The elimination of overt racism in sport has been a long-standing project among sport scholars, and we have certainly made progress in eradicating racist language within sport. But racism persists in many, mostly covert, ways, and coaches may even unwillingly contribute to this. For example, once on teams, black athletes are often asked to try-out for or are assigned playing positions that require speed and power, and they are less likely to be asked to try-out for or assigned positions that are more central to the outcome of a game – like pitching, catching or quarterbacking. Complicating this, the reproduction of black athletes as being valuable in certain positions/sports is also reproduced through black athletes themselves. Athletes from minority communities may be inspired to play certain sports or positions by existing role models in those positions. Here, a coach might help introduce them to alternative sports or encourage them to try-out for other positions.

Also, a coach's beliefs about the athletic talents and weaknesses of players from certain ethnicities may inadvertently influence the manner upon which they treat athletes. If a coach believes that white men can't jump as high as black men, or that Asian women can't swim as well as white women, these beliefs might influence a coach's training practices or motivational techniques.

Finally, racism might actually occur due to a coach's desire to include black athletes. For example, in many predominantly white areas black students are viewed as potential assets to an institution's sporting teams. Conversely, they are less likely to be seen as potential assets to debate teams, drama clubs or other intellectual or cultural pursuits. And while the focus of this chapter is on the social exclusion from sport, we must also question what disservice we may do by encouraging youth into sport and not other pursuits.

violence

Coaches often exploit their athletes' fears of social rejection, of being de-selected from playing time or not making the team the following season. 'Sacrifice' (defined here as violence against the self) becomes a part of the game because athletes (particularly those with low self-esteem or poor social support networks) are willing to risk their health through their eagerness to be accepted by their coach and peers. Thus, coaches frequently push athletes too far and sometimes knowingly have them play with injuries. In fact, research shows that over 80 per cent of the men and women in top-level intercollegiate sports (in the United States) sustain at least one serious injury while playing their sport, and nearly 70 per cent are disabled for two or more weeks (Albert, 2004).

socialising coaches into the social exclusion model

None of this is to suggest that the coach is solely responsible for all of the socio-negative outcomes of sport, but it does suggest that coaches may unwillingly reproduce these outcomes. Much of this comes from the manner in which coaches are developed and retained. Coaches are rewarded and promoted for winning, not for improving the quality of character of their athletes. As Callero (1994) suggests, and Jones, Armour & Potrac (2004) stress, coaches need to become aware of the socialisation process acting upon them so that they might utilise their agency to become role-makers, instead of just role-players. This section examines how a coach's identity is formed, and what structural forces act upon the development of that identity.

If we want to understand how a coach's identity is formed, we must first understand that almost all coaches have evolved from that of a player. The pattern holds that certain athletes find their experience in sport so thrilling they desire to participate in it for as long as possible. Coakley (1998, p. 155) says, '. . . they love their sport and will do most anything to stay involved'. Part of this is because of the sheer glory that a good athlete may experience, but also because of the prestige allotted to top-notch athletes in peer culture. Athletes (particularly in men's teams) are publicly lauded as heroes. They are honoured by their institutions and celebrated by fans (Bissinger, 1990). It is therefore understandable that from their perception sport is a socially positive vessel. Thus, athletes who are both sufficiently gifted and who exhibit the desire to follow the strict norms associated with sport are influenced to remain within them. The longer they do, and the better they are, the more likely they are influenced to promote their identity as that of an athlete (Anderson, 2005; Messner, 1987).

The process of developing one's master identity as an athlete is a product of both individual and social influences. Individually, an athlete's success might raise their sense of self-efficacy and/or self-esteem. This, of course, is likely to further a narrowing of one's devotion to sport and centres one's identity on sport. In discussing the concept of a socially perceived athletic identity with one of my university students, he said, 'When I come home from Uni, people ask me how rugby is going, not how my classes are going'. Similarly, when I asked another student what she might say to describe herself to someone she's just met she answered, 'I would tell them I was a tennis player'. The generalisation to be made here is simple: the more successful we become at sport, the more likely we (and others) are to centre our identity on being an athlete.

But centring one's identity on athleticism carries with it a measurable risk. Sport is a volatile field where careers end on poor plays or mis-steps, and athletes can be cut from a team on a moment's notice. In fact, as an athlete, the only thing that they can be assured of is that their career will end, and relative to other occupations, it will do so early. Thus, whether an athlete suddenly loses their association with their athletic identity, or whether their body ages out of competitive form, all athletes are eventually forced to disengage with competitive sport. When this happens, they are no longer valued in the sport setting (Messner, 1987).

Athletes who drop out, are forced out, or otherwise do not make the next level of sport often find themselves detached from the cultural prestige they once enjoyed – this is something sport psychologists call the disengagement effect (Greendorfer, 1992). It makes sense that athletes who were at the top of the athletic hier-archy would also feel the greatest loss upon disengaging from it. Thus, for those with no further opportunity to play competitive sport, coaching becomes one of the few avenues for getting back into the game (Lyle, 2002). Indeed, sport almost always draws leaders from those who ascribed to the previous cohort's ideals. As coaches, these ex-athletes reproduce hero–athlete narratives and promote their individual experience to inspire a new generation of athletes in the same ethos that they were once socialised into and profited from (Anderson, 2005; Hughes & Coakley, 1991).

But for every athlete who has been highly merited by sport, there are many more (perhaps thousands) who did not make the cut; often those who had horrifying experiences in sport. Yet, those who were marginalised or publicly humiliated by sports are rarely represented in coaching positions; their stories are not told in popular culture. Books are rarely published, sponsorships are not given, and movies are not produced about those who did not achieve success in sport. Even when stories of marginalised athletes are told, they normally depict a heroic underdog. In this manner, only highly selective stories are being told about sport, stories that glamorise the struggle and romance of the sporting hero genre (Stangle, 2001). These stories, fictional or real, make for great entertainment, but they may also falsely bestow the qualities upon sport that may only exist for a few. Conversely, when marginalised athletes drop out, are pushed out, or otherwise leave the sporting arena, their perceptions of how sport ought to operate are silenced. Those who were marginalised by sport or were too intimidated to play them in the first place do not go on to coach. Their stories and their ideas about how sport ought to operate go unheard. It is for these reasons that I call sport a closed-loop system. Sport is essentially closed to voices of dissent.

structural and cultural influences in creating coaches

Playing a specific sport before coaching certainly authenticates a coach. The more successful one's abilities as an athlete are, the more they are assumed to be a good coach (Lyle, 2002). In other words, athletes tend to think that a world champion athlete would make a better coach than a second-string athlete. This is because it is assumed that the journey one takes to become the worlds' greatest necessitates having as much intellectual mastery over the sport as physical. Highlighting the flaw with this way of thinking, in a discussion with one of my students, Dan reported truly liking his coach until learning that his coach did not actually play football. 'I mean I really liked the guy, he had studied the sport and knew what he was doing; but once we [the team] found out he had not played, he got no respect . . . It's like if you haven't bled for the sport, you can't know it.' This, 'I did it so you can too' narrative serves several functions. First, it prevents those not weaned on the sport from entering the coaching profession, but it also influences the system to forgo a more rigorous manner for judging the abilities of a coach. Finally, this system limits the awareness, observations or formally learned ways of thinking that others might bring to the field (like Dan's coach). If a coach learns to coach via how they were coached, does this not make the system ripe for reproducing errors?

Making the transmission of poor coaching practices easier, coaching positions, public or private, at almost all levels require no university degree in coaching, sport psychology or physical education. Certainly, a Bachelor's degree in physical education is required to teach physical education courses, but a Bachelor's in physical education is not required to coach. While many organisations and institutions may require coaching certification courses, they are generally not substantive of good coaching practices (most tend to be focused on the basic motor skills and tactics of the sport). Coaching, as a profession, stands out as odd in this matter. One cannot counsel patients without an MA or PhD, one cannot practice medicine without an MD, and one cannot cut hair without a state-certified license. Without a similar institutionalised system of training, measurement and accreditation there is little opportunity to evaluate or reform coaching practices outside of team victories, and little reason for a coach to alter their coaching style if they think it will not yield more victories.

modelling inclusive coaching

This final section is designed to help theory meet practice. Below I give a few concrete examples of how a coach might best utilise their agency to help move sport into a more inclusive direction.

choose your words wisely

The attitude that any given individual holds toward any social matter is not simply a matter of rational choice or individual agency. The attitudes one maintains towards other people, groups, or cultures are heavily influenced by a variety of factors. These include large, macro-level variables, like institutional outlooks, the organisational attitude of any given team, the influence of key team members and/or the influence of the coach.

Thus, the coach maintains at least some degree of power in shaping social attitudes among their athletes.

actively recruit marginalised people

It is a generalisable truth that most coaches seek to recruit athletes that they perceive as being capable of contributing to a team's ability to beat other teams. This is increasingly the case the further one matriculates up the ranks of sport. However, if coaches are interested in using sport to teach something other than just the value of winning, coaches might also be advised to intentionally seek individuals who represent diversity to their teams (Howe & Jones, 2006). If, for example, we believe that sport can help reduce racism by enabling white and black athletes to compete together, we must have black athletes on the team. This is not, of course, to suggest hanging a poster announcing that members of a certain race or sexuality or ability status are desired; it is, however, to suggest establishing relationships with people of these categories first and then invite them to join the team. As an example, as an American high school teacher with a top-notch team, I once invited a deaf student to run on my team. While this individual may never have thought of running on his own, the invitation thrilled him into participation, and this socialised my other athletes into a new way of understanding diversity in relationship to ability-status. Several of the athletes even learned sign language.

challenge structures that promote social exclusion

Quite simply, coaches ought to be champions of policies and practices that influence other coaches. Nowhere is this better illustrated than through the lack of coaching-influenced policies in terms of the treatment of gay and lesbian athletes. Rather than waiting for one's athletes to demand the inclusion of sexual minorities in official policies, coaches should champion this effort and mandate non-discriminatory language amongst their athletes. Coaches who organise large meets should similarly be aware of factors that may include or exclude people of disability. Simple changes often make a big difference in people's lives.

educate others

Although it may be difficult to revolutionise the way we coach without changing the structural methods upon which coaches are promoted and rewarded, it is still possible to make changes through the education of one's peers. For the most part, coaches are people with good intentions who (often) get caught up in the orthodox fervour of sport. Educating them as to the overt and covert ways that they may be producing a socially exclusive environment will help mould the whole of sport in a more progressive direction. One can, for example, give them a copy of this chapter to read. Remember, great coaches are great teachers first.

conclusion

Those who desire to make sport a more socially inclusive institution have much to work against. The structure of most sports (the way they are geared to produce winners, or the violence used to do this) necessarily limits the types and number of people who can play them. When these prohibiting structures are added to a masculine culture that values winning more than the attributes we justify playing sport for in the first place (like the development of personal character and group morale) it creates a resilient and exclusive culture for many types of people. Compounding matters, few coaches think critically about the exclusive nature of sport. This is because almost all coaches are ex-athletes that were merited by the system as it currently exists. These athletes became coaches because they were forced to disengage with that athletic identity. Thus, coaches largely continue to reproduce a system that they perceive as being effectual for many – even though it may only be so for a small minority. Even when voices of dissent exist, they are mostly silenced because of the various types of power that synergise to give a coach near-total power in his/her arena. The aim of this chapter was to first make coaches aware of the system, and then to help them be more proactive in shaping the structure and culture of sport to make the institution more inclusive.

references

Albert, E. (2004). 'Normalizing risk in the sport of cycling'. In *Sporting Bodies, Damaged Selves: Sociological Studies of Sports-related Injury*. Young, K. Amsterdam; Elsevier.

Anderson, E. (2005). *In the Game: Gay Athletes and the Cult of Masculinity*. New York; State University of New York Press.

Bissinger, H.G. (1990). *Friday Night Lights*. Reading, MA; Addison-Wesley.

Callero, P. (1994). 'From role-playing to role-using: Understanding role as a resource'. *Social Psychology Quarterly*, 57 (3), pp. 228–243.

Coakley, J. (1998). *Sport in Society: Issues and Controversies*. Boston; McGraw-Hill.

Cotter, D.A., DeFiore, J.M., Hermsen, J. D., Marsteller Kowaleski, B. & Vanneman, R. (1995). 'Occupational gender desegregation in the 1980s'. *Work & Occupations* (22), pp. 3–21.

Crosset, T. (2000). 'Athletic affiliation and violence against women: Toward a structural prevention project'. In *Masculinities, Gender Relations, and Sport*. McKay, J., Messner, M., Sabo, D. (eds.) pp. 147–161, Thousand Oaks, CA; Sage.

Crosset, T. (1990). 'Masculinity, sexuality, and the development of early modern sport'. In *Sport, Men and the Gender Order: Critical Feminist Perspectives*. Messner, M. & Sabo, D. (eds.), p. 55 Champaign, IL; Human Kinetics.

Crosset, T. Benedict, J. & MacDonald, M. (1995). 'Male student athletes reported for sexual assault: A survey of campus police departments and judicial affairs offices'. *Journal of Sport and Social Issues* (19), pp. 126–140.

French, J.R.P. & Raven, B. (1959). 'The Bases of Social Power'. In *Studies in Social Power*. Cartwright, D. (ed.). Ann Arbor, MI; University of Michigan Press.

Greendorfer, S. (1992). 'A critical analysis of knowledge construction in sport psychology'. In *Advances in Sport Psychology*. Horn, T. (ed.), pp. 201–215. Champaign, IL; Human Kinetics.

Hargreaves, J. (1993). 'The Victorian cult of the family and the early years of female sport'. In *The Sports Process: A Comparative and Developmental Approach*. Dunning, E., Maguire, J. & Pearson, R.E. (eds.). Champaign, IL; Human Kinetics.

Howe, D.P. & Jones, C. (2006). 'Classification of disabled athletes: (Dis)empowering the paralympics practice community'. *Sociology of Sport Journal*, 23(1), pp. 29–46.

Hughes, R. & Coakley, J. (1991). 'Positive deviance among athletes: The implications of overconformity to the sport ethic'. *Sociology of Sport Journal* 8 (4), pp. 307–325.

Johnson, R. (1998). *Destined for Equality: The Inevitable Rise of Women's Status*. Cambridge, MA; Harvard University Press.

Jones, R., Armour, K., & Potrac, P. (2004). *Sports Coaching Cultures: From Practice to Theory*. London; Routledge.

Kidd, B. (1990). 'The men's cultural center: Sports and the dynamic of women's oppression/men's repression'. In *Sport, Men and the Gender Order*. Messner, M. & Sabo, D. (eds.), pp. 31–45. Champaign, IL; Human Kinetics.

Kimmel, M. (1994). 'Homophobia as masculinity: Fear, shame and silence in the construction of gender identity'. In *Theorizing Masculinities*. Brod, H. & Kaufman, M. (eds.), pp. 119–41. Thousand Oaks; Sage.

Lyle, J. (2002). *Sports Coaching Concepts: A Framework for Coaches' Behaviour*. London; Routledge.

Messner, M. (2002). *Taking the Field: Women, Men and Sports*. Minneapolis; University of Minnesota Press.

Messner, M. (1987). 'The meaning of success: The athletic experience and the development of identity'. In *The Making of Masculinities: The New Men's Studies*. Brod, H. (ed.), pp. 193–209. Boston; Allen and Unwin.

Miracle, A.W. & Rees, R.C. (1994). *Lessons of the Locker Room: The Myth of School Sports*. New York; Prometheus Books.

Oxendine, J. (1988). *American Indian Sport Heritage*. Champaign, IL; Human Kinetics.

Rotolo, T. & Wharton, A. (2004). 'Living across institutions: Exploring sex-based homophily in occupations and voluntary groups'. *Sociological Perspectives* 46 (1), pp. 59–82.

Stangle, J. M. & Kane, M. J. (2001). 'Structural variables that offer explanatory power for the under representation of women coaches since title IX: The case of homologous reproduction'. *Sociology of Sport Journal* (8), pp. 47–60.

Thurow, Lester. (1985). *The Zero-sum Solution: Building a World-class American Economy*. New York; Simon and Schuster.

Whitson, Dave. (1990). 'Sport in the social construction of masculinity'. In *Sport, Men and the Gender Order*. Messner, M. and Sabo, D. (eds.), p. 55.

chapter 3
ethical coaching: gaining respect in the field

pirkko markula &
montserrat martin

introduction

Coaching is not merely about the transfer of knowledge to athletes. Coaching research has demonstrated that there are various other factors that coaches need to consider to succeed (Jones, 2000, 2003; Lyle, 1999; Potrac et al., 2002). For example, Janssen & Dale (2002) claim that successful coaches are not only the ones who win games and competitions; they are also the ones who know how to win respect from their athletes. According to these authors, the coach–athlete relationship cannot be viewed in isolation from the surrounding social network of which both the athlete and the coach play a part. In this chapter, we aim to examine one aspect of the coach–athlete relationship – respect – as shaped by social and cultural forces that surround the coach.

While we know intuitively that respect is integral for successful coaching, research in this area of coaching is scarce. We know, however, that expertise, knowledge and good methodology do not necessarily bring about players' recognition and respect for coaches (Potrac et al., 2002). A coach's skill to adapt their expertise to the demands and needs of the athlete, as well as understanding the dynamics of the surrounding situation, is fundamental in creating an effective and also an affective relationship between coach and athlete based on respect. Gaining respect in the field cannot be imposed or demanded by the coach. It has to come inherently from athletes who day by day feel an increase in their respect and trust for the coach. For a player to show and feel respect for the coach can never be a consequence or taken-for-granted as a result of the coach's power position. Nevertheless, showing respect is a legitimate way through which athletes exercise their freedom to recognise the coach's authority.

This chapter deals with the respect between coaches and players/parents. To clarify what respect might mean, we will first discuss the coach–athlete relationship as a power relationship and what this might mean in terms of gaining respect. We will then present two 'real' life scenarios where respect (or lack of it) impacts on the coaches' effectiveness. Finally, we aim to offer some advice for what coaches might do to 'earn' respect from their athletes.

the ethics of respect

While respect is an integral element of successful coach–athlete relationships, it is difficult to define what it means. It is obvious that respect exists between people and, in order to further understand what respect might mean, we need to look at such relationships more closely. Every relationship involves some use of power. Power refers to the coach's (or any individual's) ability to make others behave as they intend them to behave, to direct the behaviour or actions of another (Smith-Maguire, 2002).

In most human relationships the use of power originates from an individual's desire to advance their own cause. For example, a coach wants players to train in a certain manner or practice certain tactics to maximise the team's chance of winning. The coach's reputation and/or salary is linked to the team's perform-ance and therefore every time the team wins the coach also benefits. In many relationships power is not distributed evenly. For example, a coach's official position will put them into a power position over the players. Such an official position, however, does not necessarily bring respect from the players.

Players or parents are by no means entirely powerless in these relationships. On the contrary, players do not need to obey the coach and parents can refuse to bring their children to further coaching sessions. Smith-Maguire (2002) uses the following example to demonstrate how power relationships might work in a coaching situation:

❝Consider a coach who wants her athletes to respect a curfew. The coach can't force the athletes to go to bed at a certain time, but she can persuade them. With reference to the ill effects of sleep-deprivation or to their responsibility to be at their best for the team, the coach can convince the athletes that it is in their own interest to do as she suggests. The relation is not repressive in that the athletes ideally have the option of refusing or resisting the coach's influence. Moreover, the relation is productive, generating the ideal of (and a self-identity as) a 'committed athlete'. Positive power constrains, but is predicated on the other being able to choose; it is both restrictive and productive. (pp. 295–296.)❞

Again, respect might be one aspect that enables an effective and positive power relation. Potrac et al. (2002) affirm that the issue of power is related to the coach's need 'to gain respect of his or her charges' (p. 192). Furthermore, they claim, when a coach uses their power responsibly, his/her authority is recognised by the athletes and the coach gains the athletes' respect. In other words, the coach has gained respect through acknowledgement by the players rather than through imposing power over them (Janssen & Dale, 2002; Potrac et al., 2002). In this sense, respect is a key aspect in any coach's relationships with his/her athletes. We can conclude that respect in a coach–athlete relationship must be bi-directional as both parties have an opportunity to influence the outcomes of the relationship. While a coach's official position of authority might bestow them with more power in this relationship, the athletes can also use their power to obtain their desired outcomes. In most cases, the goals intersect, but how effectively they are achieved depends, among other factors, on the respect the coach receives from the athletes and the respect he/she gives to the athletes' power to influence the relationship.

It is obvious that power is not, in itself, evil or bad. After all, it is important that coaches control an athlete's training as they are most likely more knowledgeable about the sport than the athlete. However, it is important to consider how one uses one's power as there is considerable literature on how coaches abuse their position. For example, coaches have been found to engage in sexual harassment (Brackenridge, 2001, 1997; Cense & Brackenridge, 2001; Fasting, 2005; Fasting et al., 2004; Kirby, Greaves & Hankivsky, 2000; Leahy, Pretty & Tenenbaum, 2002; Tomlinson & Yorganci, 1997), to assign authoritative training regimes (Johns & Johns, 2002; Jones, Glintmeyer & McKenzie, 2005), to overtrain their athletes (Charlesworth & Young, 2004) or to set goals that are too ambitious for their athletes, which may lead to injury, burnout or dropout. Therefore, coaches need to consider carefully how they use their power positively to achieve their athletes' goals. As Potrac et al. (2002) note, coaches need to use their power responsibly to obtain positive outcomes and gain their athletes' respect. We use the term 'ethical use of power' to refer to positive and productive uses of power.

What might the ethical use of power mean? There is no one single answer to this question as every relationship is different and takes place in a specific social context. However, being ethical necessitates paying attention to how one uses one's power. In addition, it requires one to think about what ethical coaching behaviour might mean. Most of us do not consciously think of ourselves as users of power or of the ethics involved until we have to react to a situation when the coach–athlete relationship is not, for some reason, working. Therefore, it is important to focus on how we know about ethical coaching behaviour as we often draw from systematic knowledge to frame some actions as more acceptable than others (Smith-Maguire, 2002).

It is common to find coach education manuals or coach education courses providing plenty of information about the bio-scientific knowledge of training theory, experiential knowledge of tactics and strategy or sport psychological knowledge of planning, goal setting and motivation. In addition, some coaching manuals aim to address the ways coaches behave toward their athletes. For example, Janssen & Dale (2002) identify two types of coaches based on coaches' use of power in their relationships with athletes. *Coercive coaches* force athletes to respect them. They impose obedience by demanding respect based on their official power positions as the coaches. *Credible coaches,* conversely, believe that by establishing and maintaining credibility – justifying, reasoning, sharing coaching knowledge – they gain respect and trust. In this sense, Potrac et al. (2002) argue that power has multiple forms of expression – coercive, obedience, credibility, persuasion – but respect is only present in a few of them.

Parallel to Janssen & Dale (2002), Martens (2004) notes three coaching styles: the command style that resembles coercive coaching, the submissive style, and the cooperative style that resembles credible coaching. Martens favours the cooperative style where coaches, similar to credible coaches, cooperate with their athletes in sharing decision making over the dictatorial, commanding style or submissive, 'baby-sitting' coach who avoids making any decisions. Martens defines the cooperative coach more like a teacher who instructs how their athletes can learn to make decisions and consequently, learn how to become responsible adults. To do this, however, the coach needs to recognise their responsibility to provide leadership. Martens advocates the cooperative teacher/coach approach because this coaching style corresponds closely with what he identifies as the 'Athlete first – Winning second' philosophy for coaching (p. 33). Similarly, Armour & Fernandez-Balboa's (2000) claim that to succeed, the coach must have the ability to regard athletes as human beings first and foremost. This holistic coaching philosophy reflects the idea that coaching is a pedagogical act that acknowledges the ambiguity and complexity of the coaching context (Jones, 2006;

Jones & Wallace, 2004). This approach to coaching has been developed to expand the dominance of 'rationalistic' knowledge derived from psychology, physiology and biomechanics as traditional guidelines to coaching practice (Jones & Wallace, 2004).

We certainly agree that it is useful to approach coaching broadly as an educational enterprise because it allows coaches to think beyond the bio-scientific training of the athlete. For example, a pedagogical focus enables us to draw attention to the importance of coaching styles, the interaction and respect between coaches and athletes. But advocating this model as the best coaching style can also limit the available actions for coaches. For example, while knowing about the three coaching styles can help coaches towards more cooperation with their athletes, we are led to assume that the pedagogical approach will function equally well with all athletes and in all coaching situations. Can this really be the case? In addition, there appears to be a maximum of three coaching styles with which each individual coach should identify. For example, Martens (2004) clearly classifies coaches into three categories: commanding, submissive and co-operative. We can ask: Are there no other types of coaches in the entire, large world of sport? In addition, from these three options, we are instructed to choose the co-operative coaching style that Martens clearly prefers over other styles of coaching. When the cooperative, pedagogical style is lifted above the other coaching styles it becomes the dominant model for coaching behaviour. Instead of adding to the rationalist, scientific knowledge, the pedagogical knowledge now suppresses other ways of knowing about coaching. This way, knowledge, while perfectly useful, can turn into an authoritative model for good coaching behaviour that the coaches themselves never question. Such knowledge constructs particular attitudes towards coaching, but we believe it is important to ask whether this leads to more ethical and effective coaching?

Based on our discussion, we can conclude that knowing more about coaching – such as the bio-scientific, psychological or pedagogical aspects – can contribute to more productive coaching. However, any of these aspects can turn into a tool that dictates coaches' behaviours if advocated as the only true way of obtaining results effectively. When a 'best practice' is imposed on coaches through a singular behavioural model, it does not encourage coaches to think critically what good coaching behaviour might mean in multiple social contexts. In addition, if the 'Athletes first – Winning second' philosophy is offered as the maxim for coaching in all situations and there are no alternatives, coaches learn to accept the pedagogical coaching knowledge self-evidently as the true, correct way of knowing about coaching. Consequently, we must ask: if any coaching knowledge can turn into a tool of dominance, how do individual coaches learn to use such knowledge well or ethically? As one possible solution we aim to highlight the need for coaches to begin thinking critically about all coaching knowledge.

While there is increasing knowledge on how to coach effectively, coaching – like all human interactions – involves 'knowledge' that is not a part of either coach education texts or training textbooks. With such knowledge we mean the numerous nuances regarding people's behaviour that we somehow have to learn through everyday interactions with others. For example, we learn about power relations in any organisation or sport team through our experiences in these environments rather than from reading textbooks. While some power positions are officially mandated, such as a head coach, team manager or an owner, many additional aspects can influence people's interactions. In addition, these subtleties are often deeply embedded in societal, yet unacknowledged, belief systems regarding human behaviour. Coaches need to be aware of such 'unwritten' rules because ignoring them might severely affect their effectiveness. For example, later in this chapter we will deal with gender relations that inevitably exist when a coach becomes involved in the field of competitive sport. Tomlinson & Yorganci (1997) suggest that already complicated power relationships between the coach and the athlete turn even more complex when enmeshed with deeply engrained societal perceptions of gender roles and behaviours. While not a part of 'scientific' coaching knowledge, we learn to 'know', understand and interpret women, and men's behaviour based on mostly unwritten societal rules. These rules, while often unacknowledged or taken-for-granted, can strongly direct the coaches' behaviour yet not necessarily towards more ethical or productive coaching practice. Therefore, we ask, what does respect mean in terms of ethical coaching and gender relations?

In summary, the respect that a coach enjoys is inevitably linked to the power relations that are formed between coaches, athletes and/or their parents. In addition, these power relations are not equal, but should be positive and productive in a sense that the parties involved have a chance to influence the situation to advance their own positions. The effectiveness of these relations depends on several aspects. These include coaches' training knowledge, their behaviour toward the athletes and their coaching goals. It is important, therefore, that coaches use their knowledge in a pertinent manner to produce effective coaching. To do this, they have to actively question the knowledge they possess and also reflect on their knowledge of human relationships, such as how we know about gender, that does not exist in scientific training information. We aim to examine the ethical use of coaching knowledge, power relations and respect through two examples from real situations in coaching contexts.

example one

Place: Amsterdam
Event: Women's Rugby World Cup
Year: 1998
Setting: Spain has not played very well throughout the competition. The last game against the USA is going to take place in a few hours to decide the 7th and 8th place world rankings.

'Have you heard?' Amelia screams while tugging at the bed sheet.

I am still half asleep. Why is she so energetic? Clumsily I check my alarm clock and irritated I reply, 'Do you know it's 5.30 in the morning and tomorrow we have a very important match? I need to sleep.' Turning my body towards the wall I mutter, 'I really hope you haven't been smoking and partying. Go to bed and sleep.'

Amelia gets off my bed and goes to the toilet. I can feel she is very nervous.

I raise my head and I ask loudly with a condescending tone, 'Amelia what is going on?'

She flushes the toilet and hastily sits at the end of my bed while I raise my upper body and lean against the wall behind the bed. Cautiously she starts, 'I have been talking to Sam. You know how she has a special connection with the physiotherapist . . . and Amelia winks at me. 'Well, she went last night to his room for a "massage" on her calves and he told her that he had overheard the two coaches talking about the starting 15 for today and it seems that radical changes in the team have been planned.'

Astonished I ask, 'What do you mean?' Lowering my voice I carry on, 'Well we all know that Gloria played really badly last game as fly-half, it really won't surprise me if they put you as fly-half instead. I am sure from the training sessions they have realised that my passing is better with you than with her.'

Looking at the floor and slowly raising her head, Amelia mutters under her breath, 'No this is not the striking news.'

'So, what is it, then?' I enquire, becoming more irritated at my interrupted sleep. 'You are still on the team, aren't you?'

She answers firmly, 'Yes, but I'm playing scrum-half.'

Jumping out of bed at once I scream, '*What*?' I couldn't disguise my fury. Yesterday's image came flashing back. I saw Gloria at dinner talking to the back's coach. I thought John was implementing particular psychological skills for her concentration in today's game. I wondered why John didn't talk to both of us together, but now I see it. I am sure she blamed me for all her mistakes during the last game which we lost 43–3 and our communication didn't work very well. *What a bitch!* I think to myself. Trying to recompose myself I mutter, 'I guess Gloria is still playing fly-half.'

'No, she is not; you won't believe it, she is playing inside centre.'

Askance I enquire, 'So, then, who is playing fly-half?'

'Mary is playing. Remember Mary´s kicking form from behind was awesome against England, and then Louise goes from right-wing to full-back.'

'I see, Louise has achieved what she always dreamed,' I mutter with a malicious tone.

'What do you mean?' Amelia asks.

'Come on, Amelia, we both know that Louise can't kick; she is fast, very fast, that's for sure, but she can't play full-back in an international match. I guess this is the reward for spending all that time brown nosing. Remember that meeting that we had after that terrible training session, three days ago? Louise was making excuses for John and saying that we should be sensitive and understand that he's having a very tough time with his girlfriend.'

I pause and with irony I add, 'Who by coincidence works with Louise.'

A silence settles between us before I break it. 'I wonder if Louise is the main problem between John and his girlfriend, they have been inseparable during these two weeks.'

'Come on, Rose, don't be so bitchy. We know they are very good friends, nothing more.'

'Uh-ha, v-e-r-y good friends as you say . . . I guess . . . like Sam and Carl, the physio, right?'

Angrily, Amelia asserts, 'Unfortunately, this is another matter. Poor Sam, she is so young and naïve. Did you know she is the youngest on the team? She is 19 next month. She keeps telling me that I shouldn't worry about her, that she is fine, and that he has promised to leave his wife when we are back. What can we do about it? And you know, the problem is that he looks nice and decent, but I assure you he won't leave his wife and two kids for Sam.'

Sighing, she continues, 'I wonder if the men that are part of the team really believe in us or are we just a funny female entertainment?'

I nod agreeing and assert, 'I guess as always, we have the two sides of the coin. Some of them really believe in our improvement and performance and make a big effort in taking us further.

Look at the time Frank has spent with the forwards, but regrettably, others are more worried about their personal success among the players.'

'I guess you're right. Remember David? He only lasted with us for two months and in those two months he tried to sleep with most of us. He didn't care about the size or the age.'

Looking at her watch Amelia shouts, 'Rose! Get dressed quickly. We need to be downstairs having breakfast in five minutes.'

Suddenly the reality of the situation hits me. I had been replaced and for no apparent reason other than I was not currently massaging the coach's ego.

Angrily I reply, 'Well, apparently the coaches do not need me in the team anymore – why should I hurry?'

Disgustedly Amelia pulls my right arm and forces me to look at her. 'This is so selfish; please, don't tell me you really mean it. You know we are a team and bench players are as important as the ones who are on the pitch.'

Rejecting her hand, I respond, 'Bullshit! You say so because you have been picked for this last game. I haven't been on the Spanish team bench since I was injured three years ago. You know? It means I have played every single game.'

I start sobbing and my innermost thoughts escape before I can control myself. 'Has my rugby career come to an end? Why am I not playing?'

Amelia yells, 'Rose, please! Stop being so melodramatic. I'm sure we'll find out what all these changes are about. Trust and respect the coaches. I'm sure they have a strong motive to do what they are doing.'

After breakfast, as always before a match, we meet in the conference room of the hotel. The coaches announce the 15 players for the day's match and explain the specific tactics. Amelia and Mary are in the middle of all the tactics. I'm so jealous that I can't listen to their instructions. They do not make sense to me anymore. My mind only holds one thought: I hate Gloria and I hate John. Nobody has said anything, no surprised faces. Even John hasn't had the decency to explain to me before the meeting why I'm not playing. I have been the official scrum-half for three years; last year I was the captain and today I'm nothing. I hate rugby. My anger far outweighs my team spirit at this moment and in order to prove a point I wish with all my heart that they lose the game without me.

discussion

Early in this chapter we discussed Martens' (2004) classification of coaching styles. We can definitely recognise some aspects of the commanding, dictatorial coach in this story. The coaches make all the decisions without consulting the players whose role is merely 'to listen, to absorb, and to comply' (Martens, 2004, p. 30). Such coercive coaches (Janssen & Dale, 2002) expect players to be happy to obey and respect their decisions. These approaches can obviously lead to conflict between the players who feel that some coaches' decisions are unfair because they do not take on board players' feelings and reactions. Tomlinson & Yorganci (1997) assert that female athletes, like the rugby players in our story, prefer democratic and participatory coaching styles. Therefore, we might suggest that opting for a more cooperative, democratic and participatory coaching style, where decision-making is shared between coaches and players would improve the situation. However, is the actual solution to the issue raised here so simple?

Previously we talked about the societal attitudes on gender relations that might lead to a coach–athlete relationship and not always in a more productive direction. Therefore, our story evokes further questions that might not be answered by simply changing the coaching style. First, we would need to know why the coaches did not explain their decision directly to Rose. Was this to do, as Rose suspected, with favouring some players – the ones who had 'special relationships' with the coaches? It was also curious that Rose's roommate, Amelia, found out about the coaches' decision to change the starting line-up through a player, Sam, who had a relationship with the team's male physiotherapist, 'which is another matter', as Amelia puts it, because the physiotherapist was married with children and the players suspected him of only playing with Sam.

Clearly the female players here seem to have less power than the male characters on the team. In addition, the most 'productive' way of using power for the players is to 'brown nose' or to have relationships with the men on the team. Such use of power appears to lead to conflicts among the players themselves and, thus, does not help to lessen the dominance of the males. As a result, individual players like Rose feel that their success becomes less dependent on their performance than their ability to manage the sexual relationships in the team. Does such a use of power lead to a productive, positive use of power? Did it improve the team's performance and the players' experiences? It is clear, nevertheless, that a desire to share decision making with the players will not necessarily result in success and cannot blindly dictate the coaches' actions without becoming a tool of dominance. In our story, for example, would sharing the coaching decisions solve the problem of ethically dealing with sexual relationships within the team?

example two

Place: South-west London
Event: Last game of the under-11 football league
Year: May 2005
Setting: Aftermath of the defeat of Jack's team and the inter-action between the coach, Jack and Jack's father

'So, how much was the bribe?' shouts Jack's father as I am coming closer to the changing rooms.

I am too astounded to respond but do not want to have Jack in the middle of the crossfire. I ask him to collect the team's

T-shirts. Jack walks away, downtrodden, and I can sense he is absorbed with thoughts of the match. I should be talking and reasoning with him rather than wasting my energy dealing with another under-achieving parent who lives through the achievements of his child.

Jack walks away and his head is full of different voices – the loudest being his own! He will never be able to save up for that bike now. He should have taken that shot, but at that crucial moment he felt his loyalties split between his father and the team. His father's aggressive voice resounds in his head even now, 'Come on son you can do it yourself, be confident, you are the best.'

It should have been an easy decision to make; after all they had practiced the tactic endlessly in training. Should have been a quick play . . . two attackers on one defender . . . one always has to draw the defender in and allow your teammate to strike and score. He had felt so bad about losing that golden opportunity that he had tackled the opposing player and been handed a yellow card. Surely, though, the coach's reaction to swap him with someone from the bench was a bit harsh. They all knew he was the team's main hope of scoring and so close to the end of the match. And now their dream of travelling north next month for the English under-12 championship had completely faded away.

Trying to keep my composure, I ask Jack's father, 'What do you mean?'

'Well, for me it was pretty obvious; Jack made a mistake and you swapped him, knowing that he was the only one capable of scoring. I can see no reason for your decision other than a healthy bribe from the other side.'

During my three years of training youth football I have had to face severe criticism of my decisions and actions as a coach from players' parents, but this one had gone too far.

Calmly and decidedly, I assert, 'I'm sorry you don't agree with my coaching. But for me, at the age of 11, the most important outcome is the development of the player. That means in training sessions we practice football tactics and technical skills; likewise the respect for the rest of the team, the opposite team and, of course, referees and coaches. I might have reacted too impulsively and I should have thought twice about the repercussions of swapping Jack, but,' and I stop to take in a breathe before continuing, 'I also have to say, Mr Smith, that in the last two weeks, I have noticed a slight change in Jack's way of playing and in his attitude towards the team and towards me.' I finish my last phrase with an inquisitive look.

'Are you blaming me for something?'

We both remain silent for a minute and then he tells me, 'I've been talking to Jack about the importance of winning this game and making the finals of the championship. A friend of mine, who works in the Union, told me that this year some important technical staff from England Football will attend the event. Apparently, they are going to invest more money in promising youth next season. And I thought it was a very good opportunity for my boy.'

'Uh-ha.'

Suddenly I realise why Jack has been very selfish in training lately. He even showed his arrogance, a quality I detest in players, by thinking the team is nothing without him. Naïvely I thought all this posturing was due to the impending teenager years.

'Well, there's nothing wrong when a father procures the best for his son,' Jack's father affirms. 'Jack loves football and imitating his idols like Beckham and Owen is his dream.'

'Without a doubt,' I reply. 'But football is a team sport and if one player wants to individually succeed it unavoidably affects the dynamics of the whole team and, as we saw today, it also affects the result.'

'Today my boy was doing great until you swapped him. I'm sure the goal would have come.' Adopting a bullying attitude, Jack's father continues, 'You know something? Sometimes you force Jack to pass the ball on too much and, depending who is on the receiving end, the ball is in real danger of being lost to the other team. Like today, you told him to pass the ball to that small, clumsy boy and he couldn't keep possession.'

Feeling my anger rising, I say, 'Mr Smith, I'm not sure this is the right place or the right time to discuss the team's plans and tactics.'

'Look, son, I was on a football pitch before you were in Pampers and I know my son better than anyone in this world.' With disdain, he insists, 'Do me a favour, don't teach my lad how to play football like a pansy. He's a winner and in spite of you he'll make the England team.' His threatening voice over-whelms me and I can't answer. He continues to threaten me, 'Do you understand?'

Not knowing how to react I am completely silenced. Luckily, Jim, my support coach, waves at me and shouts, 'Pete! Can you come to the changing room? We need you here.' And without looking back at Jack's father I make my way to the changing room.

Jim says to me, 'The changing room is a sea of tears. I tried to comfort them but they are really disappointed. Any ideas?'

'Damn! I guess it is my fault.' Looking at the door and hearing their disappointment, I start hesitating about my educative prin-ciples. 'Jim, how does a coach find the right balance between education and competition in football?'

'What are you talking about?' Jim says. 'I don't think we have time now for such deep questions. Please concentrate and try to find a convincing and cheery argument before going in there.'

But before I can make a move, Jack comes out of the room and says, 'Coach, can I talk to you in private?'

'Of course,' I answer, relieved at not having to confront the team. I tell Jim, 'Try to say something positive. I'll come in as soon as I can.'

A changing room at the end of the corridor is empty. Jack and I go inside, closing the door behind us, and sit on the first bench we find. It takes a few moments for Jack to start.

'I know it is my fault!'

His eyes are welling up when he continues.

'I know I should have passed that ball to Matthew and I didn't.' He stops and says thoughtfully. 'My father said I had to forget about the rest of the team, that they are rubbish.' A tear rolls down his cheeks and, raising his voice, he asserts, 'This was my game!' Recomposing himself, 'He said that if we got to the finals I could make the English team for the next year, he has a friend somewhere who could help me get a grant from the Union. I was going to win this for him. Did you know my dad nearly made it on to the English team when he was my age and then he had a knee injury?'

Now I am getting really angry – my innermost fears have been affirmed. I was having a firsthand experience of the age-old story of a parent living through his child.

'And . . .' Jack continues.

There was more; confused, I look at Jack and ask, 'And . . . ?'

'He also promised . . .' Looking at the ground and refusing to meet my glare, he ashamedly mumbles, 'He also promised me a new bike if I was the one scoring the goals in the team.' Jack bursts into tears.

Feeling completely devastated, I don't know whether I should be comforting him or telling him off. A million and one thoughts race through my mind, I had heard of parents bribing their children to do better, but Jack? I lower my head between my knees and feeling I can't repress my emotions any longer, I scream. 'Shit, Jack, shit . . . why?' I also want to cry.

Jim knocks on the door. 'Pete, will you come soon? I really need you in there.' I get up in silence and, walking towards the door think, *What the hell am I going to tell to the rest of the team?*

discussion

In this narrative, the coach's situation is very complex. It is difficult to locate his coaching style within the categories provided by Martens (2004). In one sense, the coach seems to have a very good relationship with his players. For example, Jack feels comfortable enough to explain his situation to his coach. Therefore, the coach cannot be classified purely as a commanding dictator who expects his players to quietly obey orders. During the game, the coach also appears to be able to make decisions when it comes to player selection and strategy, and therefore he is not merely there to baby-sit his players as a submissive coach would do. Finally, the coach seems to have been able to teach his players to be responsible for their actions as Jack openly confesses how his actions led to losing the game. Therefore, the coach obviously cooperates with his players. Opting for a 'better' coaching style does not appear to solve the situation as the coach already adopts a cooperative style as advocated by Martens (2004). The coach in this story already acts like a teacher, but his pedagogical approach does not ease his problems. What to do, then, when players' parents get involved? What to do when players are placed between the differing understandings of what is important in the sport by the coach and a parent? And lastly, what to do when a parent clearly loses respect for the coach's opinions and ways of coaching in front of his child?

In youth sport, coach–parent relationships are not easy. On the one hand, it is necessary to have parents involved with sport to support their children's development. On the other hand, parents who are too involved tend to manipulate their children's experiences. In this example, there was a clear discrepancy between Mr Smith's goals for sport and the coach's goals for sport. Jack was, at some level, aware of both sets of goals, but could not successfully negotiate his position between these two influential figures in his life. He was left to wonder if winning at all costs was the priority in football? Or was sport about being part of a team and considering the benefits for all the team members before one's own success? We can ask if such a negotiation should be a child's responsibility anyway? The coach's situation is also difficult as he is responsible for a team rather than an individual athlete. Jack's failure, thus, failed the entire team. Jack's father's example would affect the other parents' responses to the coach's ideals and the team performance.

It is also notable that the coach tries to solve the conflict situation entirely by himself. He speaks to Mr Smith, he listens to Jack and he is to explain the situation to the rest of the team. While the assistant coach is trying his best to help, the actual responsibility falls entirely on Peter, the head coach. Based on our earlier discussion of power relations, Peter has plenty of power and, therefore, takes the responsibility for the events. How do the power relations between the coaches on this team really work? Should they share power more effectively? Neither coach, however, seems to know how to handle the situation. Could they not have anticipated this type of conflict with the parents?

Peter's position should lead a coach to ask: what is the role of sport for the children I am coaching? And also, what is the role of sport for the children's parents? Most coaches tend to overlook parents' views because parents are not at the field during training sessions. In addition, some parents are more difficult to deal with than the children. Sometimes power relationships between a coach and a parent are not clear because of the age difference. In this example, Jack's father is older. He considers himself more qualified than the coach and dismisses the coach's actions in front of Jack. In this situation it is clear that the aim of improving Jack's development is betrayed by adults – the coach and the parent.

In this example we have also included 'bribing' as the trigger for Jack's confusion and then highlighted the negative consequences of his behaviour. 'Bribing' a player or an athlete is not new in sport. For instance, some footballers get 'rewards' from their clubs or Unions if they score goals in important matches. This is comparable to 'bonuses' for breaking world records in others sports, which is considered an acceptable practice for improving performances. Therefore, it might not be altogether surprising that some parents view 'paying' for their children's good performance as entirely acceptable. However, the intricacies of such individual rewards within team contexts are potentially problematic. Unavoidably, Jack's father's 'bribing' has affected Jack's performance and behaviour with the coach and the rest of the team. Here we return to the notion of ethics in sport: how do coaches decide what is ethical, good sportsmanship in the current commercial world of sport? How do coaches influence parents' attitudes in addition to children's attitudes about the nature of competition in sport? Questions such as these cannot be resolved simply by the coach following the 'best practice' or coaching style.

conclusion

The examples in this chapter show what can happen in everyday coaching situations. Some coaches never face these types of situations, but they might confront numerous other problems deriving from the relationships between their athletes, the athletes' parents or the national and international level administration of their sport. In these situations, the unethical, dominant use of power often plays a major role. It is evident that each coaching situation is different depending on its cultural context and the individuals involved. As the examples demonstrate, ready-made categories, such as coaching styles, while clear-cut, can turn into limitations when we try to understand complex everyday situations with multiple ways of acting, reacting and knowing about sport. In most cases, an unquestioned and categorical reliance on previous knowledge will not necessarily ease problematic coaching situations. Instead of just coping with the highly problematic incidents, the coaches should seriously consider the actual causes for the conflict by asking, what went wrong?

In the case of the rugby team, Rose's development as a player could have definitely been improved by a more constructive handling of the decision to drop her from the starting line-up. While our example concerned only one player, and it could be argued that her reaction was only one individual case, we do not know how many other players on the team faced a similar situation due to undemocratic decision making. A more open decision-making process might also reduce the players' feeling that the most effective way to advance their career is to enter into a relationship with one of the male personnel on the team. However, altering the coaching style might not automatically change the way power is used by the female players and the male coaches. Nevertheless, it appears obvious that the sexual politics within the team creates conflicts that do not advance the team's performance or promote respect between the players or between the coaches and the players. Consequently, some action would be required to eradicate the issues deriving from the sexual relations within the team.

In the case of the football team, the benefits of different ethics seem even more tangible. In the current situation, all parties involved are left with anger and confusion. The coach does not know how to deal with the situation at all. He has just 'lost face' in front of a parent and has lost control over one of his player's behaviour. The player is confused about what to do, feeling upset about losing his bike and guilty about letting down both his Dad and the team. Mr Smith has no respect for the coach, is disappointed with his son's performance and has no plans to change his rather disruptive behaviour. Something needs to be done if the football team is to continue to function at the required level.

Consequently, at this point, the coach needs to establish what constitutes ethical coaching behaviour in a particular, troublesome situation: how can one behave differently in this situation? This is by no means a simple task and requires quite a lot of thought from the individual coach. However, to work through this situation coaches might want to begin by defining their ethics as situational: different styles might work in different situations with different individuals. In addition, in this chapter we have discussed how respect derives from the ethical use of power by the coach. In the beginning of the chapter we defined power as a way of obtaining one's goals. For example, some coaches might want to behave ethically to be respected by their athletes, but others might, first and foremost, want to obtain results and aim to behave ethically to maximise that goal but minimise the harm to the athletes and to themselves. Consequently, each coach needs to clearly define their ethical goals and be clear about them to their athletes. This requires that the coach and the athletes clearly articulate and agree upon such mutual goals. In some cases, defining ethical coaching requires first defining the aims for the coach–athlete relationship and then thinking how these goals can be maximised. By such goals, we don't only refer to long- and short-term training goals, but to a larger understanding of why the coach and the athlete are involved in sport. While different coaches can have different aims, all these can be achieved through ethical means if they are transparent to the coach, the athletes and the parents. It is evident, in any case, that more effective coaching requires critical reflection of problematic coaching situations and more openly defined individual coaching ethics.

references

Armour, K. & Fernandez-Balboa, J.M. (2000). 'Connections, pedagogy and professional learning'. Paper presented at CEDAR 8th International Conference, University of Warwick.

Brackenridge, C.H. (2001). *Spoilsports: Understanding and Preventing Sexual Exploitation in Sports*. London; Routledge.

Brackenridge, C.H. (1997). '"He owned me basically": Women's experience of sexual abuse in sport'. *International Review for the Sociology of Sport*, 32, pp. 115–130.

Cense, M. & Brackenridge, C.H. (2001). 'Temporal and development risk factors for sexual harassment and abuse in sport'. *European Physical Education Review*, 7, pp. 61–80.

Charlesworth, H. & Young, K. (2004). 'Why English female university athletes play with pain: Motivations and rationalisations'. In *Sporting Bodies, Damaged Selves: Sociological Studies of Sports-related Injury*. Young, K. (ed.), pp. 163–180. London; Elsevier.

Fasting, K. (2005). 'Fight or flight?: Experiences of sexual harassment among female athletes'. In *Feminist Sport Studies: Sharing Joy, Sharing Pain*. Markula, P. (ed.), pp. 129-145. Albany, NY; State University of New York Press.

Fasting, K., Brackenridge, C. & Sundgot-Borgen, J. (2004). 'Prevalence of sexual harassment among Norwegian female elite athletes in relation to sport type'. *International Review for the Sociology of Sport*, 39, pp. 373–386.

Janssen, J. & Dale, G. (2002). *The Seven Secrets of Successful Coaches*. Tucson, Arizona: Janssen Peak Performance.

Johns, D.P. & Johns, J.S. (2000). 'Surveillance, subjectivism and technologies of power: An analysis of the discursive practice of high-performance sport'. *International Review for the Sociology of Sport*, 35, pp. 219–234.

Jones, R.L. (2006). 'How can educational concepts inform sport coaching?' In *The Sports Coach as Educator: Re-conceptualising Sports Coaching*. Jones, R.L. (ed.), pp. 3–13. London; Routledge.

Jones, R.L. (2003). 'Constructing expert knowledge: A case study of a top-level professional soccer coach'. *Sport, Education and Society*, 8, pp. 213–229.

Jones, R.L. (2000). 'Toward an applied sociology of coaching'. In *The Sociology of Sport: Theory and Practice*. Jones, R.L. & Armour, K.M. (eds.), pp. 33–43. London; Addison Wesley Longman.

Jones, R.L., Glintmeyer, N. & McKenzie, A. (2005). 'Slim bodies, eating disorders and the coach-athlete relationship: A tale of identity creation and disruption'. *International Review for the Sociology of Sport*, 3, pp. 377–392.

Jones, R.L. & Wallace, M. (2004). 'Another bad day at the training ground: Coping with ambiguity in the coaching context'. *Sport, Education and Society*, 3, pp. 329–342.

Kirby, S., Greaves, L. & Hankivsky, O. (2000). *The Dome of Silence: Sexual Harassment and Abuse in Sport*. Halifax; Fernwood.

Leahy, T., Pretty, G. & Tenenbaum, G. (2002). 'Prevalence of sexual abuse in organised competitive sport in Australia'. *The Journal of Sexual Aggression*, 8, pp. 16–37.

Lyle, J. (1999). 'The coaching process: an overview'. In *The Coaching Process: Principles and Practices for Sport*. Cross, N. & Lyle, J. (eds.). Oxford; Butterworth-Heinemann.

Martens, R. (2004). *Successful Coaching*. Champaign, IL; Human Kinetics.

Potrac, P., Jones, R.L. & Armour, K. (2002). '"It's all about getting respect": The coaching behaviours of an expert English soccer coach'. *Sport, Education and Society*, 7, pp. 183–202.

Smith-Maguire, J. (2002). 'Michel Foucault: Sport, power, technologies and governmentality'. In *Theory, Sport & Society*. Maguire, J. & Young, K. (eds.), pp. 294–314. Oxford; Elsevier.

Tomlinson, A. & Yorganci, I. (1997). 'Male coach/female athlete relations: gender and power relations in competitive sport'. *Journal of Sport and Social Issues*, 21, pp. 134–155.

part 2
coaching in practice

bowes, bates, avner

chapter 4
communicating with athletes

imornefe bowes

introduction

Consider how many times the following statements or sentiments can be heard at a training facility.

⁶NO, not like that! How many times do I have to tell you?⁹
⁶What are you looking at? I told you to watch . . .⁹
⁶I've told you before, what don't you understand?⁹
⁶How many times have I told you⁹

Many coaching texts describe the importance of communication in coaching and present a more or less straightforward account of steps to follow when communicating with athletes; these, as anyone who has coached will agree, often seem far from the reality of the task. This chapter will provide some ideas for coaches to consider in their interaction with athletes and present a view of communication that is centred on developing shared understanding during communication. The main argument in this chapter is that communication is about developing a shared meaning between coach and athlete through the creation of collective knowledge (d'Arripe-Longueville et al., 2001) instead of seeing communication as transferring knowledge from one person to another.

The creation of knowledge occurs as a result of individuals processing information from both current and past experience through activation of individual schemata (Bartlett, 1932). Adopting this view of communication presents additional demands to both the coach and athlete in terms of awareness of self and other, and challenges the simplified view of communication as a straightforward transfer of ideas. Further, this chapter will outline an often cited (Martens, 2004) model of communication, and examine some possible uses of communication before considering the concept of schema (Bartlett, 1932) in an attempt to provide some insight into potential factors that can affect coaching interactions. More specifically, this chapter will suggest how the dynamic quality of the schemata held by a coach or athlete can guide the way they construct their reality. The impact of this is how coaches and athletes communicate, understand their roles and develop expectations of each other.

a model of communication

In sports coaching literature, guides to communication present ideas of verbal and non-verbal communication, active listening and voice characteristics as being influential during coaching interactions. Few, it seems, tackle the mechanics of why communication works, instead citing factors that help avoid communication breakdowns (Athanasios, 2005). Such guides build on a traditional (stemming from cognitive psychology) account of communication as outlined below:

The communication process (Martens, 2004):

1 The individual has thoughts they wish to convey.
2 The sender then translates thoughts into a message.
3 The message is channelled (usually through spoken words but sometimes through non-verbal means, such as sign language) to the receiver.
4 The message is received.
5 The athlete interprets the message dependent upon comprehension.
6 The receiver then responds internally, such as being interested, getting mad, feeling relieved, and so on.

Martens' (2004) process as depicted above details how one person creates, encodes and transmits a message to a receiving individual; it doesn't, however, draw attention to the interaction inherent in the process. Anecdotal evidence from coaches seems to confirm that, while talking with an athlete, they are very conscious of their behaviour which affects how they proceed in the interaction. For example, noticing slight changes in athletes' mannerisms might lead to truncation or adaptation of the interaction, thus highlighting the interactive nature of communication. This awareness stresses the importance of the contextual information supporting messages when sent and received, as contextual information is attributed to non-verbal or para-verbal methods of communication (gestures, facial expressions, proximity and even the physical appearance of the communicator). Contextual information can tell the receiver about the intent of the sender; however, detection of these messages requires interpretation. Issues can arise as people can express conflicting messages verbally and non-verbally, resulting in a possible basis for misunderstanding.

This need for interpretation provides a possible site of hidden interaction present in the previous model of communication (Martens, 2004), as para-verbal and non-verbal communication require awareness by the receiver in order to be effective. Consider the athlete who has just been benched against their opinion. Think about their gestures and mannerisms; coaches have to interpret these and decide on the message the athlete is sending. Sometimes non-verbal messages can over-ride the verbal message. Many sports coaching texts do not outline the mechanics of how this interpretation occurs, which would provide a real insight into communication; this will be addressed in the remainder of this chapter.

As previously cited (d'Arripe-Longueville et al., 2001) the creation of collective knowledge relies on both parties (athlete and coach) taking part in the activity. In Martens' (2004) model the 'other' person is the receiver; for their part, active listening is professed to support effective communication. While they attend to the main content of the message they accompany this attention with relevant non-verbal messages. Active listening therefore suggests interest and understanding to the sender; however, in certain coaching situations this does not mirror the nature of coach athlete interactions (Lenzen et al., 2004). Research on communication within sports highlights a number of barriers (Athanasios, 2005) which confound communication between coach and athlete. Often these aspects are what the receiver is dealing with and bases responses on instead of sending associated supporting contextual information. The importance of non-verbal communication has been highlighted by research (Martens, 2004) which contends that it makes up 70 per cent of all communication. Therefore, as active listening involves mostly non-verbal methods of communication, any lack of continuity can confuse or create barriers within the process.

uses of communication

Some authors (e.g. Weinberg & Gould, 1995) argue that communication can be used for a number of purposes such as persuasion, evaluation, information, motivation, etc. Other uses have been researched and might not be so obvious, but nonetheless, can be invaluable to coaches trying to understand why communication doesn't seem to be effective. Within coaching the most obvious use of communication is for feedback and instruction; other uses see it employed with little inherent meaning and more focused on the sub-text. A discussion of this latter application of communication will show how it can complicate interaction in coaching.

communication as a source of feedback and instruction

As a source of feedback, communication has been addressed by many researchers in a number of situations (for a more detailed discussion see Cassidy, Jones & Potrac, 2004), typically focusing on the most effective content, timing and amount in relation to skill development. Few address the possible negative impact that continual coach feedback can have on athletes' ability to take feedback from the physical experience of the activity. New coaches should remember that skill development does not take place outside the context of the game (Light & Fawns, 2001), therefore verbalisations need to be related to the physical experience of the game to help connect the sequenced physical activities. As Light & Fawns (2001, p. 73) state, 'This allows us to see the continuity between the reasoned articulations of play and students' corporeal engagement in it'.

Although verbal feedback from the coach can be a form of knowledge of results (KR) or knowledge of performance (KP), both are considered augmented feedback, which is defined as 'information provided to a learner from an external source that describes the outcome of a performance and/or the quality of performance' (Rose, 1997, p. 265). Another class of feedback is intrinsic feedback which is immediately available to the performer as it comes from sensory receptors as a consequence of movement (Fischman & Oxendine, 2001).

Consider the following scenario; a player attempts a new skill under the supervision of the coach and fails. Immediately the coach feeds back either knowledge of results, 'Unlucky, that serve was just long', or knowledge of performance, 'You didn't throw your elbow up enough on your serve'. Both examples can provide very useful information to the athlete; however, the danger is that this focus on an external source of feedback (coach communication) can create a dependence on the coach and the verbal or cognitive aspect of the skill. Therefore what is important to consider is when and how often to give feedback, as some research (Janelle et al., 1997) suggests that performance can be improved if feedback is only given when sought by the athlete, as opposed to augmented feedback accompanying every trial.

Where recent research suggests that instruction makes up over 50 per cent of the speech of a coach (Gallimore & Tharp, 2004), consider this in light of suggestions that cognition – within sports performance – is underpinned by the 'levels of physical, chemical, biological and social interaction and upon bodily and affective forms of involvement' (Light & Fawns, 2001, p. 75). Such thinking could be aligned with constructivist ideas highlighting the mutual involvement of agent, activity and world within learning. Citing Lave & Wenger's (1991) arguments challenging the reductionist 'exclusively in-the-head' process of cognition stresses the importance of a participation framework. Thus, being quite critical of a focus on higher mental experiences being given priority over physical experience, where talking about the skill, is deemed more important than the physical act and feedback from performing the skill.

I would suggest that there is a tendency at novice coaching sessions to provide the largest part of feedback through verbal communication rather than plan for it to be made explicit in the activities. This can be problematic as coaching has arguably become a verbal experience, and lessened the necessity to retain a physical medium as a primary focus of communicating understanding within sports coaching (Light & Fawns, 2001).

In summary then, communication in traditional models depicts the successful transfer of a message (often in coaching information about performance) from one person to another. However, this is often found to be significantly different from the practice of communication in coaching. Here we see coaches repeatedly conveying the same information, either on subsequent attempts or subsequent occasions, which suggests that the message has not been transferred successfully or received accurately by the athlete. The information available to coaches to improve this practice focuses on the type and frequency of communication in relation to athlete performance and skill learning. What is suggested in this chapter is a move away from psychologically or pedagogically fixed approaches to coaching (Cassidy et al., 2004; Jones & Turner, 2006) to a consideration of more constructivist ideas in relation to the activity. This move could be expressed by a move towards a relational (acknowledging interaction) account that attempts to reflect the interaction between coach and athletes during coaching (Bowes & Jones, 2006).

the meaning behind the words

As discussed, communication can occur for a number of reasons with a host of research dealing with when, how much, and what to give in communication; as a coach, how you use this information will in some ways define how you approach interacting with athletes (Martens, 2004). Maybe less discussed is the subtext of the message. Consider this example:

❝Kathy, you are too anxious on the strip. You are telegraphing messages to your opponent as to what your intentions are. Relax, see things develop, trust your decisions and actions, and when you see the window of opportunity open up, go for it! In addition, fence with confidence, keep your focus, and remember to take it one touch at a time.❞ (From Yukelson, 2001, p. 138.)

When analysing this communication, we can see there is nothing verbal coming from the athlete. Would we then count this as another coach monologue to/at an athlete, or is there meaning just in the interaction? In situations like this, it can be important to consider the subtext of the message; no doubt a visual account of the preceding moments would show astute coaches non-verbal signals from the athlete that call out for some form of support. Therefore, the content might be of less importance than the meaning it embodies.

People understand the world by creating meaning through interpreting signs (Saussure, 1974), which leads to the creation of something that is personally meaningful. Adopting a constructivist approach[1] researchers in educational settings suggest that

[1]Theorists argue that learners learn by interacting with their environment and processing information based on their experiences, as opposed to one individual being responsible for filling them with knowledge (behaviourist approach, Good & Brophy, 1986).

children learn how to behave at school during early experiences; here they learn how to respond to teachers' instructions and the meaning of being at school. Similarities can be drawn within the coaching setting as young athletes learn behaviours from older athletes; they learn the meaning of sport from their early experiences, which help shape how they communicate and understand their part in the activity. Moreover, they also create an understanding of the roles of the people involved, for example, coach, athlete, parent, etc. The concept, inter-subjectivity (Göncü, 1993), is used to describe how shared meaning is developed amongst participants within an activity; examples of this can be seen in the language used in all sport settings. Athletes use phrases to describe actions, concepts, plans, anything that helps them jointly navigate their current situation. By considering how these two aspects, developing shared meaning and learning of behaviour, interact during coaching, a lack of inter-subjectivity can lead to miscommunication.

Research by Göncü (1993) describes how in schools the responsibility for learning is taken away from children and given to adults. Again we can see this mirrored in traditional accounts of the coaching process where the coach's role is created as having responsibility for the athletic development of the athlete. The impact of this is that athletes and coaches do not develop the same meanings for activities or, at times, hold the same goals for activities within the coaching setting. This results in differing perceptions or understandings between coaches and athletes about behaviours and actions.

Consider the example where a coach states that a certain athlete does not see the impact of mistakes as the athlete continually makes them during practice. Now the same athlete, who actually does not have confidence in a newly developed technique, continues with sub-standard attempts and therefore makes mistakes in drills. Another reason could be that the athlete has not grasped the aim of the practice and so performs the skill without the required focus. In this example we can see how differing positions within the same activity can be interpreted differently. The coach sees the responsibility for change as dependent on the athlete complying with their requests and sharing the same understanding of errors. Whereas the athlete perceives it as the coach's job to design the drills and correct their technique through feedback; if they participate in the drills then they perceive that they are doing what the coach has requested. These examples, although they may not seem to deal with communication directly, do specifically result from a lack of shared meaning, which in this chapter is the essence of communication.

To understand roles, instructions and drills requires navigation of a social setting, which, it has been argued, individuals achieve through activation of schemata (Fiske & Taylor, 1984). Applying schema theory (Bartlett, 1932; Fiske & Taylor, 1984) to explain the basis of the coach–athlete interaction can provide both the perception of individual agency that is apparent and a site for the complexity of communication during coaching. Various terms have been used to describe this specific aspect of cognitive psychology, for example, frames, scripts, plans. Although not identical they are related closely enough so that discussion of one will hold most of the prominent aspects of the area. In this section I will discuss schemata (singular being schema).

Cognitive psychology regards individuals as 'constructive thinkers', continually searching for causes and inferring meaning of behaviour, and acting on the basis of this knowledge (Snyder et al., 1977). The most basic element of this behaviour has been argued to be schemata (Rumelhart, 1980) which are data structures for representing concepts stored in memory. Although quite a dated concept, the strength of schema theory (Bartlett, 1932) is that it provides insight into the way knowledge is represented and used during comprehension and inferences; as such it is argued to allow an interlocking between the environment and the mind, positioning knowledge as actively constructed. Basically, schema theory is a theory about knowledge, how it is represented and how this representation assists in the use of knowledge (Rumelhart, 1980). Discussion of this concept in the following section is abstract, in parts not making direct reference to coach–athlete communication. However, in the concluding section it will be built on and details given to suggest schemata directly impact on the communication process.

schema theory

Within schema theory, meanings are stored as *prototypes*, normal situations or events that best illustrate concepts. An example of this could be 'football player' or 'coach'; this will automatically create a picture in your mind. You are aware that this is not the *only* football player or coach ever to exist, but it comes with a set of guesses (inferences) about how they look, act and maybe even sound. These inferences allow you to predict or to shape how you think you would interact with them. To allow for the myriad of situations that could be encountered, schemata not only contain exact details, but they also contain variables (non-defined aspects that allow expression in a number of different environments). These variables allow adaptation within the application of schema, so they become skeletons around which situations are interpreted. It is perhaps most valuable in that it is abstract, so it can be applied in many different contexts, therefore schemata contain both aspects of the concepts and relationships between aspects (Fiske & Taylor, 1984). This knowledge about aspects (variables) and their inter-relationships are called *variable constraints*, which can serve two functions; to help identify the role of qualities in the situation (in a coaching situation, there is a perception of what a coach is/does) and then as *default values*. Best guesses about that concept (that the coach would be the person giving feedback on technique) can often be used as the bases of role expectation/stereotypes. With these aspects in mind it can be seen how schemata can be used to help construct understandings of situations. Specifically, in communication they can form the basis of the content between coach and athlete. This can be further complicated if we consider how stereotypical roles (default values) can affect what we expect from individuals. This added element of complexity in the simplified model of communication offered by some coaching texts implies that there might not be a direct transfer of concept, but actually to communicate the exact idea could be quite tricky. Within a coaching context this could potentially explain why coaches need to enter into dialogue with athletes or repeat themselves so often, not because the players aren't listening, but because it takes multiple attempts to generate a shared understanding of a concept with both coach and player.

schema and communication

The following section will focus on how schema can influence communication through three aspects of schema theory; how they shape memories of experiences, guide perception of events, and generate assumptions or inferences about situations.

Schema can be thought of as a network of points and connections. The activation of thoughts occurs following identification of external stimuli through perception. Conceptually this is described as *instantiation*, where a particular set of values is found in a particular set of variables at a certain point in time

(Rumelhart, 1980). It is this *instantiated* schema that forms memory traces in response to physical experience. So we hear a new coach (a variable) give critical feedback (a value) to another player (another variable) during a match (positioned in time). This instantiates the schema of our old coach who we remember as being short-tempered and over critical. The academic discussion of schema and memory seems to focus on what will be remembered (stored in memory) and why. Researchers (Neuschatz et al., 2002) have reported equivocal findings about the effect of schema and memory. Specifically, assuming that unexpected or incongruent information is more likely to be remembered as it doesn't 'fit' with the instantiated schema, in other words we remember the unexpected.

The resulting task is to try to get unexpected information to fit into the current situation, to understand it. Consider the old coach previously mentioned; if they were to suddenly give floods of positive, supportive feedback the athletes would recall it but also have to search for a reason to explain the change. It is worth noting that this suggested view of memory, instead of being a passive storage of information, now becomes an active process that is guided and influenced by the current environment. Events that fit with an instantiated schema become mundane and when we are asked to recall this information we often actually tell of the typical event, the prototype schema, not an exact account of what occurred. This view affects communication when both coach and athlete have pre-existing schema. The consequence is that they don't necessarily remember what occurred but rather take some of the information and substitute the rest with default values of their schema.

The subsequent impact of adopting this view of memory is that schema can organise incoming information thematically, in other words our prior knowledge allows us to decide what information is relevant in a given situation (Fiske & Taylor, 1984). So how are these schemata activated? One approach to this has been described as 'top-down' or conceptually driven activation (Bobrow & Norman, 1975), where expectations lead individuals to focus on particular details of the environment. Supposing you were told that an athlete had a bad attitude before you met them, this could lead you to perceive confidence as arrogance or see their questioning as some form of disrespect; an inference that could be different if alternative schemata were activated before the meeting. Once a schema has proved moderately successful it becomes the basis for prediction about unobserved events, meaning that we do not need to have witnessed all aspects of a situation before we will make an assumption (Rumelhart, 1980). The single behaviour of the new coach that mirrors that of an old coach tells us what to expect in future interactions/communications. As a result of the flexibility of a schema, only the semantic (the meanings) and relational components of concepts are encoded. This suggests that interpretation of new information hinges on its congruence with the schema active at that time (Nassaji, 2002).

Perception in this model is partly dependent upon the schema that has been activated, a second process of activation is 'bottom-up' or data-driven. Here, upon detection of a number of features, a higher order schema is activated to lead to perception of a concept; Rumelhart (1980) contends that theses processes are not distinct but work in tandem during the perceptual process. Thus, the dynamic quality of schemata can be seen in the ways they are proposed to represent knowledge, through selection, abstraction, interpretation, integration and reconstruction (Alba & Hasher, 1983), guiding the perceiver to actively construct reality. Communication then becomes the complex process of all parties simultaneously involved in making meaning of physical experiences. This process includes individuals' experiences and current perceptions of the situation, which might or might not be shared (Göncü, 1993).

The preceding information about schemata might seem very interesting to cognitive psychologists, but how does it affect coaching and, specifically, communication? Consider a typical interaction between coach and athlete: athlete performs, coach feeds back, athlete listens, maybe some dialogue between them and the athlete performs again. While discussing communication we need to consider the development and impact of roles (which in this encounter are implicit), for example who is responsible for what? The athlete perceives the coach as the person whose job it is to evaluate the performance; the coach regards the athlete as the person they have to give knowledge to about the performance. These roles and relations are contained in schema and when employed these provide a cognitive map, (containing self, other and inter-action scripts) that have been constructed over repeated exposure to similar contexts. This is how past social experiences affect current ones thus presenting a more complicated picture of communication.

Researchers argue that individuals perceive the world 'through the filter of their person schema' (Baldwin, 1992: p. 462), aligned to social situations. Baldwin further contests that a person's perceptions emphasise the influence of the perceiver's schema in the formation of impressions of others. Particularly, (Baldwin, 1992) schemata led participants to report particular aspects of information at the expense of others and recall preferential information that is highly consistent with the active schemata. So before the coach has opened their mouth the athlete has already activated schemata or is actively searching for features to establish an understanding of the up-coming interaction. This cognitive activity of the athlete can colour any message the coach gives, or in some cases maybe further, the athlete interprets the body language of the coach as a non-verbal message and then reacts accordingly.

In this view of communication the coach might not have intended or sent the message the athlete has interpreted, which is in fact a remnant of previous experiences of the athlete. Recalling the suggested importance of non-verbal communication as being 70 per cent of all communication (Martens, 2004) the potential impact of schema becomes crucial. Previously mentioned person perception becomes significant, as Fiske & Taylor (1984) describe personality traits as a type of information that is relevant and consistent with a particular type of person, and related goals specify the 'person-in-situation' category which denotes specific intent. These qualities are easily accessible in memory as prototypic traits and prototypic goals which are rich in content and useful for predicting behaviour in a particular setting. The degree to which these aspects of schema impact on the interpretation and selection of information becomes apparent considering how much past experience is bound up in typical interactions (Bobrow & Norman, 1975), thus arguing that the majority of athletes have stereotypical views of what coaches want and why they communicate with athletes. Often this comes from early experiences where coaches are viewed as authority figures and communication is mainly about praise or scolding (Martens, 2004). Technical feedback means 'I'm doing it wrong and coach is not happy', or if coach doesn't comment it means that coach didn't notice or 'coach doesn't like me, and doesn't think I'm worth the time'. If the reader does not perceive these as typical responses, it would be interesting to think about past experiences and their perception of 'the coach' as the basis of this schema. Although this places a great deal of significance on past experience, research (Baldwin, 1992) suggests that individuals can become hyper-vigilant about attending to behaviours that can be interpreted as indicators of specific qualities these being derived during past experiences.

This attentional specificity is equally applicable to perception of self as Markus and Kunda (1986) contend that individuals go to great lengths to verify their self-conceptions and structure their environment to generate more self-confirming information. In a coaching context this is the athlete who always interprets feedback negatively as their self-concept may contain negative components, 'I can't do this', 'I've never been good at this'. These suggestions highlight the impact of perception and role development in shaping communication between coach and athlete.

possible solutions

Having identified some aspects that impact on communication, how can they be integrated into coaching practice? The following section contains some suggestions for the implementation of the ideas presented in this chapter; essentially an application of existing constructivist thinking (Light & Fawns, 2001) should facilitate this move for practitioners.

video-stimulated recall

Something as simple as video-taping coaching sessions and replaying them with athletes can provide a method of developing shared understanding. Video-stimulated recall – used in teaching, nursing and counselling (some functions typically attributed to a coach) – involves video-taping passages of behaviour and replaying it to participants, which allows them to report their concurrent cognitive activity. Although some researchers stress the possible problems with this method of research (*see* Lyle, 2003), in a practical application it can be very effective in providing an 'objective' account of interaction. This account provides the basis for both parties to explore and express their understanding of each other's activities and the meanings they attribute to them. This process will help to highlight perceptual and inferential differences providing an insight into an individual's schema as their basis of interactive decision making (Housner & Griffey, 1985). Research (Saury & Durand, 1998) shows coach/athlete interactions are not solely a result of planned structures, but are mediated by the temporal aspects of the environment and the related expectations of each party. Therefore the impact of schema on the expectations of others will be illuminated in this process.

performance profile

Butler (1989) and Butler & Hardy (1992) proposed this as a method of allowing insight into the perceptions of both athlete and coach as, 'the coach/psychologist can make astute observations about the athlete's performance from, as it were, "outside", whereas the athlete is the only one who can comment on the performance from "inside"' (Butler, 1995; p. 34.). Performance profiles consist of a visual display of the aspects athletes perceive as important in attaining a top performance, against which the athlete maps their self-assessment. This map provides an opportunity for the athlete to reflect on what they perceive in the role, while also enabling the coach access to the 'inside' of the athlete's perception of the world. Why is this important? For two reasons; research suggests that athletes' perceptions of a coach's effectiveness are tied to their expectations, and shared understanding of a role is a major influence on the production of that role. What an athlete expects affects their perception of the coach's behaviour, thus the coach's ability to perform the role effectively (Kenow & Williams, 1999), an area not often highlighted for new coaches.

evaluation

Generally cited as an important component in the development of a coaching programme, evaluation occurs allegedly without coaches really being aware of the criteria involved (Barber & Eckrich, 1998). Where typically a win–loss record has been the basis of evaluation, questions (Gorney & Ness, 2000) have been raised regarding the validity of this as the ultimate measure. Recognising this, research (Gorney & Ness, 2000) has identified categories of competencies coaches should possess interesting, proposing, 'It is usually the areas of interpersonal relationship skills and conceptual skills that tend to be impediments to the success of coaches' (p. 49). Therefore evaluation should attempt to gather information to clarify athletes' perceptions of coach behaviour in relation to these measures. As Kenow & Williams (1999) posit, perception and meaning given to behaviours are more important in defining attitude and actions towards the actor than the behaviour itself.

Similar to an educational context (MacPhail, 2001) athletes' voices don't seem to be heard in an evaluative context within coaching, where multi-source evaluations have been argued (Barber & Eckrich, 1998; p. 303) to 'increase the credibility of the performance review, as well as the communication'. Such findings suggest the need for a method that would allow athletes to contribute to the data generated during an evaluation. Nominal Group Technique[2] (NGT) is an interview process where individuals work independently in the presence of peers who will encourage self-disclosure among participants, as responses are not given verbally. Following a discussion the statements generated around the desired outcome are ranked jointly by the participants, which allow an equal voice for all involved. Employing such a method during an evaluation of coaching would allow an insight into the meaning held by athletes. Furthermore, it can be used as a basis to measure development of the communication process of a group, thus showing the emergence of shared understanding.

---

[2]As a detailed account of Nominal Group Technique is outside the scope of this chapter refer to MacPhail, (2001) for a fuller discussion.

conclusion

I feel by this point that the reader should be in a somewhat Catch-22 situation, with more questions than answers. If all this chapter has done is to introduce some new concepts, words or phrases in relation to communication, then in some way it has been worthwhile. Although many might claim that they have effective communication skills, I would argue that no one really has a surefire way of ensuring effective communication. Gallimore & Tharp (2004) studied the coaching techniques of John Wooden (the most successful coach in NCAA Basketball in terms of wins) and recounted details of his effective communication style. Deeper inspection of his coaching practice revealed that his interaction was at the end of an intricate, meticulous process of planning and learning about his athletes. Hopefully this discussion of communication and some related concepts will assist in the exploration of this process.

references

Alba, J.W. & Hasher, L. (1983). 'Is memory schematic?' *Psychological Bulletin,* 93, pp. 203–231.

Athanasios, L. (2005). 'Communication problems in professional sports: The case of Greece'. *Corporate Communications: An International Journal,* 10, (3), pp. 252–256.

Baldwin, M.W. (1992). 'Relational schemas and the processing of social information'. *Psychological Bulletin*, 3, pp. 461-484.

Barber, H. & Eckrich, J. (1998). 'Methods and criteria employed in the evaluation of intercollegiate coaches'. *Journal of Sport Management*, 12, pp. 301–322.

Bartlett, F.C. (1932). *Remembering*. Cambridge; Cambridge University Press.

Bloom, G., Stevens, D., Wickwire, T. (2003). 'Expert coaches' perceptions of team building'. *Journal of Applied Sport Psychology*. 15, (2), pp. 129–143.

Bobrow, D.G. & Norman. D.A. (1975). 'Some principles of memory schemata'. In *Representation and Understanding: Studies in Cognitive Science*. Bobrow, D.C. & Collins, A.M. (eds.). New York, Academic Press.

Bowes, I. & Jones, R.L. (2006). 'Working at the edge of chaos: Understanding coaching as a complex, interpersonal system'. *The Sport Psychologist*, 20 (2), pp. 235–245.

Butler, R.J. (1995). *Sports Psychology in Action*. Oxford; Butterworth-Heinemann.

Butler, R.J. (1989). 'Psychological preparation of Olympic boxers'. In *The Psychology of Sport: Theory and Practice*. Kremer, J. & Crawford, W. (eds.), pp. 74–84. Leicester, British Psychological Society.

Butler, R.J. & Hardy, L. (1992). 'The performance profile: Theory and application'. *The Sport Psychologist*, 6, pp. 253–264.

Cassidy, T., Jones, R.L., & Potrac, P. (2004). *Understanding Sports Coaching: The Social, Cultural and Pedagogical Foundations of Coaching Practice*. Routledge; New York.

d'Arripe-Longueville, F., Saury, D., Fournier, J. & Durand, M. (2001). 'Coach-athlete interaction during elite archery competitions: An application of methodological framework used in ergonomics research to sport psychology'. *Journal of Applied Sport Psychology*, 13, pp. 275–299.

Fischman, M.G., Oxendine, J.B. (2001). 'Motor skill learning for effective coaching and performance'. In *Applied Sport Psychology Personal Growth to Peak Performance*. Williams, J.M. (eds.). New York, McGraw-Hill.

Fiske, S.F., & Taylor, F.E. (1984). *Social Cognition*. New York; Random House.

Gallimore, R., Tharp, R. (2004). 'What a coach can teach a teacher, 1975–2004: Reflections and reanalysis of John Wooden's teaching practices'. *The Sports Psychologist*, 18, pp. 119–137.

Göncü, A. (1993). 'The development of inter-subjectivity in social pretend play'. *Human Development*, 11, pp. 327–344.

Good, T.L. & Brophy, J.E. (1986). *Educational Psychology: A Realistic Approach*. New York; Holt, Rinehart and Winston.

Gorney, B. & Ness, G.R. (2000). 'Evaluation dimensions for full-time head coaches at NCAA division II institutions'. *Journal of Personnel Evaluation in Education*, 14, pp. 47–65.

Housner, L.D., & Griffey, D.C. (1985). 'Teacher cognition: Differences in planning and interactive decision making between experienced and inexperienced teachers'. *Research Quarterly for Exercise and Sport*, 56, pp. 45–53.

Janelle, C.M., Barba, D.A., Frehlich, S., Tennant, L.K. & Cauraugh, J. (1997). 'Maximizing performance feedback effectiveness through videotape replay and self-control learning environment'. *Research Quarterly for Exercise and Sport*. 68, 4, pp. 269–279.

Jones, R.L. and Turner, P. (2006). 'Teaching coaches to coach holistically: The case for a Problem-Based Learning (PBL) approach'. *Physical Education and Sport Pedagogy*, 11, pp.181-202.

Kenow, L., Williams, J.M. (1999). 'Coach–athlete compatibility and athlete's perception of coaching behaviors'. *Journal of Sport Behavior*, 22, pp. 251–260.

Lave, J. & Wenger, E. (1991). *Situated Learning: Legitimate Peripheral Participation*. Cambridge; Cambridge University Press.

Lenzen, B., Brouwers, M., Dejardin, B.L., Lachi, B., Cloes, M. (2004). 'Comparative study of coach–athlete interactions in mixed traditional Japanese martial art, female amateur track and field, and male professional basketball'. *International Journal of Sport Psychology*, 35, pp. 77–90.

Light, R., Fawns, R., (2001). 'The thinking body: Constructivist approaches to games teaching in physical education'. *Melbourne Studies in Education*, 42, (2) pp. 69-88.

Lyle, J. (2003). 'Stimulated Recall: A report on its use in naturalistic research'. *British Educational Research Journal*, 29, (6), pp. 861–878.

MacPhail, A. (2001). 'Nominal group technique: A useful method for working with young people'. *British Educational Research Journal*, 27, pp. 161–170.

Markus, H., & Kunda, Z. (1986). 'Stability and malleability of the self concept'. *Journal of Personality and Social Psychology*, 51, pp. 858–866.

Martens, R. (2004). *Successful Coaching*. Champaign, IL; Human Kinetics.

Nassaji, H. (2002). 'Schema theory and knowledge-based processes in second language reading comprehension. A Need for Alternative Perspectives'. *Language and Learning*, 52, pp. 439–481.

Neuschatz, J.S., Lampinen, J.M. Preston, E.L., Hawkins, E.R., Toglia, M.P. (2002). 'The effect of memory schemata on memory and the phenomenological experience of naturalistic situations'. *Applied Cognitive Psychology*, 16, 6, pp. 687–688.

Rose, D. (1997). *A Multilevel Approach to the Study Motor Control and Learning.* Boston, Allyn & Boston.

Rumelhart, D.E. (1980). 'Schemata: The building blocks of cognition'. In *Theoretical Issues in Reading Comprehension*, Spiro, R.J., Bruce, B.C. & Brewer, W.F. (eds.) pp. 33–58. New Jersey, Lawrance Erlbaum Associates.

Saury, J. & Durand, M. (1998). 'Practical knowledge in expert coaches: On-site study of coaching in sailing'. *Research Quarterly for Exercise and Sport,* 69, pp. 254–266.

Saussure, F. de (1974). *Course of General Linguistics.* London; Fountana.

Snyder, M., Tanke, E.D. & Berscheid, E. (1977). 'Social perception and interpersonal behaviour. On the self-fulfilling nature of social stereotypes'. *Journal of Personality and Social Psychology*, 35, pp. 656–666.

Weinberg, R.S., & Gould, D. (1995). *Foundations of Sport and Exercise Psychology.* Champaign, IL; Human Kinetics.

Yukelson, D. (2001). 'Communicating effectively'. In *Applied Sport Psychology: Personal Growth to Peak Performance.* Williams, J. (ed.), pp. 135–149. Mountain View CA, Mayfield.

chapter 5
coaching experience, coaching performance

iain bates

introduction

The term experience is one that is synonymous with a variety of working cultures (Schon, 1983) including coaching (Gilbert & Trudel, 2001). The importance of this concept is echoed throughout the emerging literature underpinning coaching. This is highlighted by scholars who have recently suggested that the coaching process is infinitely complex and constructed around social experiences and exposure to the working context as much as explicit facts detached from the reality of the real-life coaching environment (Jones et al., 2004; Jones & Wallace, 2005; Saury & Durand, 1998). As a consequence of such findings, it would appear that experience, and perhaps more importantly individuals' interpretations of their experiences, represent pivotal factors for coaches in developing their coaching knowledge. Such work has re-enforced the need for individuality and a body of knowledge for each practitioner that is representative and reflective of circumstances and realistic for the coach in action.

The aim of this chapter is to identify how coaches can use their own experiences in a constructive manner using experiential learning theory (Schon, 1983). Here, the concept of reflection will be explored to understand how coaches can construct a practical and dynamic knowledge base with functional validity for the specific coaching context. The intention here is to recognise that reflection is not only an academic tool, but one that with time, thought, consideration and experimentation can be effectively used to elevate the practice of each individual coach, regardless of their position or status. In terms of structure, I will begin with an overview of experiential learning. Having done so, I will present two practical working examples of reflection aiming to break down the barriers which prevent the widespread implementation of this process as a core competency of coaching practice.

But first let me introduce myself. I am currently working as a Performance Tennis Coach based at the University of Bath. My job focuses on the specific development of five elite junior players and I am responsible for their technical, tactical, mental and physical development. I have been in this role for two years. I find coaching children both very challenging and very rewarding. Coaching players aged between 12 and 16 provides an enormous opportunity to influence their development as both players and people. Prior to my role in coaching I played tennis full time and was something of a journeyman around the satellite circuit. My most prominent success came as a student; when working towards my Coach Education and Sports Development degree I won a gold medal at the World University Games in Daegu, Korea. My degree gave me the opportunity to explore a number of contemporary issues surrounding coaching, notably the impact of experience on the construction of coaching knowledge.

a relationship between experience and performance?

In the contemporary literature supporting coaching and coach education, it is apparent that coaching is essentially an idiosyn-cratic process that is embedded in the working context of each practitioner (Jones et al., 2004). It is evident that experience plays a key role within coaching performance due to the limi-tations of coach education (Jones & Wallace, 2005) and the development of knowledgeable coaches (Jones et al., 2004). It would appear in many cases that that the reputation and experi-ence of a successful coach precedes their professional qualifications and as a consequence their 'stock' is greatly increased and their reputation enhanced compared to the coach with little formal experience. It can be deemed, then, that exposure to a certain environment over time, as both an athlete or as a coach, allows knowledge to be constructed that is implicit in nature and practically relevant for the coach in their own working life (Saury & Durand, 1998).

This knowledge base is dynamic and constantly evolving as new events and incidents are encountered. Such exposure to the working context allows routines and practices associated with coaching to develop so more and more situations and actions become familiar to the coach as their experience grows. Consequently, it could be argued that through their experiences, coaches construct a working understanding that allows them to recognise and understand key events that they can then draw upon and disseminate effectively in the set context to deliver successful coaching practice. In turn, their performance is enhanced as they become more confident and able to deal with important situations in the environment in which they work.

Although the connection between experience and performance appears to be very strong, it would be inappropriate to make the assumption that a coach simply constructs knowledge through 'being there' with numerous authors rightly suggesting that experience is no guarantee of knowledge (Gilbert & Trudel, 1999; Saury & Durand, 1998). This can be highlighted when you consider the evolution of many sports in the current era. In tennis, for example, the men's game has been revolutionised by players such as Roger Federer and Rafael Nadal. As this current generation continues to alter the boundaries of acceptability, the coaches' expectations of the requirements for players to achieve success have also moved with them. Therefore, as a coach an awareness of such moves must remain at the forefront of your mind because simply drawing upon your own experiences in times past, as a player or a coach, is not conducive to helping players develop the appropriate armoury to succeed in the modern game. Therefore, it would appear that it is how this experience is used which distinguishes its relative value from an educational perspective. This concept is widely recognised in other professional domains (Schon, 1983) where the impact of experience and the construction of domain-specific knowledge has been analysed and formulated into experiential learning theory.

experiential learning theory

The following section will identify the key concepts associated with Schon's (1983) experiential learning theory and made applicable to coaching by Gilbert & Trudel (2001). Although it is recognised that there are other theories, this is considered to be the most relevant and appropriate as it has been made specific to the ·construction of knowledge in coaching. The purpose of this review is to outline the key stages that need to be undertaken to allow coaching to be analysed and considered methodically through a structured framework of practice thus ensuring important information is gleaned and constructively used to enhance coaching performance.

Despite the concept of experience being inherent both within this paper and experiential learning theory, it would be inaccurate to think that every experience encountered will result in knowledge being constructed. Coaches are exposed to a diverse and multi-faceted range of events and issues that are not always directly applicable to them. Thus, for an occurrence to become live it must be consistent with the individual's beliefs and how they perceive their coaching role. Such an image could be formed as a consequence of an individuals' coaching habitus (Bourdieu, 1990) or their coaching philosophy.

A coaching philosophy is made up of core values and beliefs, which help shape and guide practice. Coaching philosophies often refer to a coach's stance on areas such as winning versus participation, short-term against long-term success, team spirit versus individual progress in addition to areas such as sports-specific progress, discipline and personal development. This self-constructed means of gauging the significance and educational value (or lack of it) of each encountered experience is called the role frame (Schon, 1983). This allows coaches to make themselves more receptive to coaching issues that are congruent with their own beliefs. To help demonstrate this point, here is a short paragraph from my own coaching philosophy:

❝ My ultimate goal in coaching is to develop independent, pro-active decision makers who embrace their development as a challenge. Through hard work, endeavour and enjoyment I encourage players to maximise their potential ensuring that they have no regrets about missed opportunities in performance sport. Seeing a highly motivated player giving everything is as satisfying for me as an important victory. In the words of the great iconic coach Vince Lombardi, 'winning isn't everything – but making the effort to win is' . . . '

As a consequence of this philosophy, I have often encountered situations where maximum effort and commitment towards a specific objective are below expectations. This was especially prevalent at the beginning of my coaching career when I simply believed that by telling somebody to work harder they would. This naïve assertion was quickly quashed when athletes failed to respond to such hollow statements. Following the 'role frame' principle, such incidents became coaching issues directly within the parameters of my philosophy that I needed to overcome, through experience, to improve my practice.

reflection in experiential learning theory

Having successfully constructed the issue for exploration, the next stage is to uncover meaning by examining the issue and entering a phase of reflection. Reflection is an everyday concept at the heart of the experiential learning process that symbolises a level of thought or deliberation about a particular topic. At a more structured level, and within this theoretical framework, reflection is an inter-connected process combining in-depth thought with purposeful action that acts as a mediator between experience and knowledge (Gilbert & Trudel, 2001). Through consideration and analysis of the factors that led to an unanticipated or unplanned event, such as a teaching strategy or the structure of a practice, the coach is able to break down a problem and challenge the validity of their action or behaviour in a specific situation. This allows a connection to be made between the cause and the effect, allowing the experience to be analysed and understood. However, simply establishing causation is only half the process and for this to be developed into a learning experience an individual must interpret this relationship as an issue in practice that needs to be overcome by considering alternative strategies and testing them through action (Moon, 1999).

Embedded within the reflective act then, the phase of 'testing' is a vital cog as it allows the coach to explore alternative methods of practice and consider solutions to the encountered incident that are not simply reproduced as a course of habit. Despite the desire and bravado of many coaches it is essential to recognise that the coach cannot hold all the answers to all novel coaching problems all the time. In their pioneering model of experiential learning in coaching, Gilbert & Trudel (2001) proposed six options for generating strategic alternatives to problematic situations. Two of these were inwardly focused with the coach's existing repertoire combined with their creative thought reported as important tools for solving problems. A third option was the use of coaching materials, where the coach is able to draw upon static resources to formulate solutions. The final three options (reflective transformation, joint construction and advice seeking) focus on gleaning new information through observation (reflective transformation) or seeking support from colleagues (joint construction) or specialised expert coaches (advice seeking). Although this list is not exhaustive it provides a conceptual framework that illuminates an array of options for dealing with irregular occurrences. The components of these proposed strategies will be explored further through the practical examples later in the chapter.

Once alternative strategies are generated they must be tested and evaluated through experimentation, either in the real or the virtual world. It is important to recognise the importance of this stage for two reasons. First, without it proposed strategies cannot be tested and thus problematic situations cannot be solved. Second, it distinguishes purposeful reflection from basic trial and error. From personal experience, when you first attempt to reflect upon your practice it is hard to differentiate between the two. This is because through trial and error you reach a point where you elicit the intended result in your coaching and therefore you feel you have achieved the desired outcome. However, the significant difference is that trial and error is an isolated action where no consideration of the factors, which have led to the intended result, are identified or recognised. Using this method you simply try one way, then another and then another until eventually you are successful. Consequently, you are unable to recognise the relationship between the key factors which led to the desired outcome. This means that this process has no functional validity outside the isolated action which it helped to solve. In contrast, through reflection you are able to piece together the component parts and understand their relationship. Therefore, you are able to recognise certain characteristics within future problems that you recognise and act upon from previous experience.

Having undertaken such experimentation, the final stage of the cycle is to evaluate the results. Here the coach must consider the effectiveness of any experiment undertaken in light of the problematic occurrence. A successful evaluation will result in the termination of the reflective conversation. However, if a negative outcome is elicited the practitioner must formulate an alternative strategy again and continually repeat this process until a positive outcome is achieved. Hence, on completion of this cycle, the coach is armed with new knowledge which is practically applicable and constantly evolving. This helps to facilitate purposeful and considered behaviour where potential consequences are evaluated resulting in conscious and evidence-based learning and action in the working environment.

issues to consider

Despite the logical presentation of this theory in abstract terms, it would be wrong to believe that this is a straightforward and problem-free act that can be universally applied as a routine element of practice. Notably, it takes time, willingness and an open mind to embrace the process of reflection within a daily routine. A consistent barrier inhibiting the success of reflection in coaching is the emotional and subjective elements of practice. As much of the literature tells us, coaches are often socialised into accepted methods of practice through exposure to their own coaches in their formative years and through the conceived structural limits placed on coaching practice as a consequence of social expectation. Therefore, practice is often reproduced and seen as successful by force of habit without due consideration as to why. To break down this barrier and to challenge the assumptions underpinning delivery, coaches must recognise and understand that being critical of personal practice is not ego damaging but a core competency of evolving professional knowledge. Thus, despite the difficulties that we face in being critical we must remain active rather than passive practitioners, able to consciously choose alternative methods and strategies to suit our needs.

Furthermore, delimiting key events and analysing the relevant aspects of the encountered experience is challenging even for an advanced reflective practitioner in the unpredictable world of sports coaching. Yet to provoke in-depth reflection, recorded occurrences need to be vivid and resonant (Wildman & Niles, 1987). Therefore, collation of the appropriate data in the midst of action can be a challenging task. Indeed, many practitioners, especially at the outset, consider the events that have taken place in isolation without analysing the more critical factors which have contributed to the unintended consequence. Although personal observations are very important to understand events, it is essential to consider the help and support that others can give you when gathering the data from an encountered event. It is likely that fellow coaches, parents, helpers and players can provide valuable data to enrich your understanding of what took place. Using these options should not be seen as second best as you can not expect to piece together all the pieces of the jigsaw in the instant the event takes place.

This highlights that the coach is not an isolated figure burdened with the expectation of improving personal practice alone. Experiential learning in many ways is a relational process. As long as you are eager to seek the input and critical analysis of others, a process coaches often take personally, you are able to create a network of valued individuals who are able to help you understand events encountered while coaching. This extends to the athletes, because for the coach to understand the impact of their actions on the performer they need to be spoken to, listened to and encouraged to be honest to ensure a holistic understanding of an issue. Failing to seek their opinions or to observe their responses or to seek their views devalues the impact they can have in helping you to understand a situation in its totality. Engaging with the athlete in this way does not undermine you as a coach, as some of the literature suggests, it simply allows you to understand the impact of your coaching behaviour on the athlete with the view to improving your practice.

reflection and experiential learning theory in the coaching context

Despite the reported benefits of using experiential learning theory to enhance coaching practice, there is still a low uptake of coaches who engage in such a process on a regular basis. There remains an undercurrent of feeling amongst coaches that academic theories are not for them because they are disconnected from reality and impractical in the context in which they work (Bates & Jones, 2005). The next section of this chapter will present two everyday coaching issues in an attempt to demonstrate how the reflective process can be fused with everyday matters that are specific and important to you, the coach. The first example focuses on coaching style while the second relates to issues surrounding the construction of a training programme for adolescents.

example one

Following a period of technical development Frank, the coach, doesn't believe that his pupil fully understands the areas of his action that need improvement. Despite communicating these in a variety of ways, utilising his favoured teaching method of verbal instruction, Frank is getting frustrated and can't understand why progress is so slow. Having discussed this with his athlete, Frank discovers that the learner feels confused and has lost sight of what he is trying to do because he perceives that the coach is giving him too much instruction verbally.

The potential for the coach to 'affectively educate' the individual is a primary motive for many coaches. Initiating a change in behaviour or a change in knowledge leading to rapid improvement is the ultimate objective for many in our profession. However, to do this effectively the coach must be able to perceive, evaluate and reflect upon the actual impact of their adopted coaching style on inducing such change. The need for such 'practical' reflection is evident in the example above with the coach's favoured methodology proving to be ineffective with the learner.

The challenge for the coach here is to consider whether his pedagogical actions have been a limiting factor in the learning of the pupil. An important first step to help decode events would be to draw upon session plans and session evaluations to examine planned and actual modes of delivery, together with their effectiveness during practice. Such documentation could be complemented with the thoughts and opinions of the athlete. Merging these two sources of evidence would allow key issues for investigation to be delimited. In this case, it would seem that the learner has become confused by the information they have been presented with through the coach's preferred method of verbal interaction.

In response to these findings, the coach must seek to determine why such practice has been adopted, the strengths and weaknesses of it, and challenge any pre-determined assumptions guiding his work. To help facilitate this process there are a number of models available in the literature. Figure one highlights three questions for structured reflection. Using pre-determined questions can be useful to help signpost the coach to the heart of the issue allowing in-depth thought and prompting learning that might not otherwise take place.

figure one: questions for structured reflection

1 What was I trying to achieve?
2 Why did I intervene as I did?
3 What were the consequences of my action for myself and the person I was coaching?

(Adapted from Johns, 1994.)

For this questioning to be effective the coach must be open-minded and respond with honesty. What should emerge from this example is recognition by the coach that, despite trying to induce performance enhancement, simply using one dominant method of instruction can be limiting. Merely drawing upon your preferred method of intervention rather than considering alternatives can lead to confusion, lack of understanding and limited learning, which appears to be the case here. Therefore, the coach must determine the origin of his practice and consider whether this strategy is being implemented because it is most effective or because it is the default way of disseminating information in an educational environment. Despite the difficulty in doing so, answering such key questions will help the individual to assess the merits and value of his practice raising issues for investigation through consideration of alternative methods. To structure the process of considering alternative strategies the coach might like to consider the questions outlined in figure two.

figure two: questions for considering alternative strategies
1   What other choices did I have?
2   What could be the consequences of these choices?

(Adapted from Johns, 1994.)

Asking such questions at this stage of the process enables the coach to consider alternative options for delivering the message ensuring that unsuccessful coaching behaviour is not ignored. Furthermore, it allows creative analysis to take place ensuring that the impact of different strategies is considered from the learners' point of view. This allows coaches to draw upon and be creative using their existing knowledge contained within their own coaching repertoire. Here, the coach could call upon alternative teaching strategies including visual or kinaesthetic methods such as video analysis or old way/new way demonstrations.

To develop these ideas further, the coach could observe others in action to see how they present information to their athletes in different ways. From my own experience I have found watching and learning from other coaches to be an essential part of my informal education. For example, when I first saw a colleague do a split-screen video presentation using computer software I immediately wanted to know how I could do the same. Therefore, I asked them to show me how to undertake such a process. Asking colleagues for help and advice like this highlights the potential benefits of working in coaching teams. I am fortunate enough to work with five excellent coaches and we are constantly talking and sharing ideas about how certain scenarios can be effectively dealt with.

Having accepted that a new teaching method is required, the idea of using video analysis to present the information would be valid here and the coach must experiment with this in practice. The conclusions of this experiment can, of course, only be speculated upon, but it is possible that by being shown something as opposed to being told it immediately the coach is being imaginative and thoughtful in his delivery as opposed to monotonous and predictable. This could capture the athlete's attention in a new way, enabling them to appreciate and understand what the coach is asking them to do instead of being bored and confused. Should it be unsuccessful, the coach would need to re-visit their strategic options and re-try until a positive outcome is achieved.

To summarise, this process has allowed the coach to challenge any assumptions underpinning his behaviour in a quest to find better and more effective ways of doing things. This results in the coach learning new strategies to use in future practice. In reality, there are many alternative strategies to communicate a message. However, as coaches we often get trapped in our own preferred method rather than considering the way the individual will learn best. Although there are many learning style inventories available, these are not commonplace in the coaching world; consequently coaches should perceive themselves as 'adaptive practitioners' who, through reflection, become armed with the appropriate knowledge to perform a variety of coaching strategies that resonate and meet the needs of their learners (Hargreaves, 2001).

example two

As a coach working with elite child athletes, Joan is incredibly aware of her moral and ethical obligation to coach her subjects safely and in line with long-term development guidelines. However, she has only recently taken up her position working in this situa-

tion as she has been used to working with senior players who are training full time. Since her arrival she has transformed the training programme so it resonates with her own expectations. It comes as a great surprise to her when the parents of one of the children claim that she is pushing their child too hard, training the children like adults and consequently risking the potential for burnout. They are demanding that she pulls off and reduces the volume and intensity of training.

Much work has been undertaken in the field of long-term athlete development and although these informative guidelines have their critics, they provide a structural framework to guide training prescription for adolescents. Coaching elite youngsters can be a complex process as parents or carers are able to challenge and question what the coach is doing as a consequence of the moral, social or ethical obligation that is owed to them.

The main coaching issue for analysis and reflection here is to consider whether the prescribed training programme is appropriate for the context. Although the training programme has been constructed with the best intentions in mind, for the coach it must be remembered that children are not mini-adults and you cannot simply impose an adult training programme on young athletes. Therefore, it must be considered whether the coach's intervention in re-structuring the training programme is expecting too much and risking burnout or overtraining or if it is, in fact, right on target.

As a vital first step the coach would need to collate all the relevant information relating to the training programme. This would include the frequency, volume and intensity of training against an annual plan, a ratio of technical, tactical and physical work, a ratio of training weeks to competitive weeks, training logs, and diaries and medical information including growth rates. This would provide objective data to compare with published guidelines. Having collated this data the next stage would be to read some journal articles about coaching adolescents in an attempt to confirm the key issues. It would also be important to do some sports-specific research, both via the internet and through personal coaching materials, to read about the suggested training loads that are relevant to the sport in question.

In this example, 'coaching materials', both personal and researched, become an essential resource to enable the coach to collate the key facts relating to the coaching issue. The theoretical concepts outlined in the coaching resources have served as an informative guide to assess the nature of the training programme. Although there appears to be a stigma attached to such resources by coaches (Bates & Jones, 2005), the wealth of academic and vocational information available is excellent and, as this example demonstrates, practitioners should not hesitate to use such information when seeking to either clarify issues or to generate solutions to complex problems.

Having collated the appropriate data, the coach would be required to conduct a virtual world experiment to determine whether the parents have a point or if the programme is exactly how it should be. In doing so, the results could produce either a positive or negative result. If the experiment highlighted that the programme was placing too great an expectation on the athletes the coach would need to re-examine the components of the programme and seek alternative solutions in schedule design. In contrast, a positive result demonstrating training loads within published guidelines, with sufficient rest and regeneration phases together with growth and training load correlation minimising the risk of overuse injuries, would validate and reinforce the quality of programme being delivered.

However the experiment is concluded, there are important contextual lessons in addition to the practical ones to be learnt from this experience. Primarily, the coach needs to be aware that the impact of her work goes outside the immediate coaching act and in this working context key stakeholders need to be informed about why certain things are happening through ongoing communication. To be effective here you must be constantly aware of their expectations and manage a relationship where key people are informed of why certain tasks and practices are being undertaken. This would eradicate the potential for speculation to arise about the merits of practice. Recognition that this process is in stark contrast to working with senior players, where reasons for certain events are explained and interpreted directly by the athletes, is vital. This experience would also reinforce the need for training programmes to be well thought out and grounded in relevant theory. These lessons gleaned from the encountered incident effectively demonstrate the coach becoming more knowledgeable of the working context, allowing modifications to be made to her own practical knowledge base.

conclusion

While it is recognised that much of what has been written about in this chapter requires time, thought and deliberation we are at a stage in sports coaching where we, as a body of professionals, need to take responsibility for our own development. If coach educators are finding it hard to integrate the concept of ambiguity and the ever-changing social dynamic that typifies the coaching environment (Jones & Wallace, 2005) into formal coach education then we as coaches must recognise this and take responsibility for ourselves. It is hoped that the discussion in this chapter will provide a means for you to do this: 'knowledge for action' cannot be spoon fed, thus, it is your prerogative to construct your own working reality that has the appropriate impact in your own context.

It is envisaged that this chapter has brought to life the concept of reflection and elevated the significance of this practice as an integral component of the coaching process. It is with hope and anticipation that the barriers minimising the impact of this tool, within the coaching fraternity, have been broken down. Essentially, reflection is a practical act that coaches can undertake. It is not an inaccessible tool only for educated intellectuals; it is a relevant mechanism for developing coaching knowledge. Indeed, the process of reflection could be viewed as a method of continuous professional development (CPD). Throughout the contemporary literature on CPD in either coaching or education, it is clear that there is a shift from traditional to reform methods of this process. The more traditional approach treats CPD as a function of professional practice rather than a mechanism to allow new knowledge to be constructed that is real and relevant for the working context. The latter is gaining increased momentum in terms of value in professional development. Indeed, the National Foundation for Educational Research in the UK found that CPD is most effective when teachers have autonomy over the choice and direction of their personal development (NFER, 2001). Consequently, through experiential learning, coaches are able to set issues for development that directly resonate with their own practice. From here, coaches can seek the answers to the issues, both themselves and through the help of others, as outlined in the reflective process above, rather than attending workshops or courses as a means to fulfil license obligations.

Although this chapter has outlined a variety of important issues, the most important message is simply to take part in reflection at some level. As a coach, the barriers preventing us from undertaking this process are real, yet we need to recognise that to develop and promote our own position in the coaching environment we need to be constantly open to new ideas, new concepts and receptive to lifelong learning. By taking the time every day to consider 'why did I do that?' you will enable yourself to understand at a greater level the rationale and thought underpinning your practice. This will allow you to evaluate the validity of it in context, promoting greater thought and, in time, the evolution of considered, well-thought and well-delivered coaching practice.

references

Bates, I. & Jones, R. L. (2005). 'The making of an expert coach: The construction of coaching knowledge'. Conference paper presented at the Exercise Science, Sports Medicine and Sports Psychology Symposium at Cardiff University, 24 June 2005.

Bourdieu, P. (1990). *The Logic of Practice*. Oxford; Blackwell.

Cushion, C. J., Armour, K. M. & Jones, R. L. (2003). 'Coach education and continuing professional development: Experience and learning to coach'. *Quest*, 55, pp. 215–230.

Gilbert, W. & Trudel, P. (1999). 'Framing the construction of coaching knowledge in experiential learning theory'. *Sociology of Sport On-line*, http://physed.otago.ac.nz/sosol/v2il/v2il.htm

Gilbert, W. & Trudel, P. (2001). 'Learning to coach through experience: Reflection in model youth sport coaches'. *Journal of Teaching in Physical Education*, 21, pp. 16–34.

Hargreaves, D. (2001). 'A future for the school curriculum', www.qca.org.uk/ca/14-19/dh_speech.asp

Johns, C. (1994). 'Nuances of reflection'. *Journal of Clinical Nursing*, 3, pp. 71–75.

Jones, R.L., Armour, K. & Potrac, P. (2004). *Sports Coaching Cultures From Practice to Theory.* London; Routledge

Jones, R. L. & Wallace, M. (2005). 'Another bad day at the training ground: Coping with ambiguity in the coaching context'. *Sport Education and Society,* 10 (1), pp. 119–134.

Moon, J. (1999). *Reflection in Learning and Professional Development: Theory and Practice.* London; Kogan Page.

NFER. (2001). *Continuing Professional Development: LEA and School Support for Teachers.* National Foundation for Educational Research (NFER) (2001). Slough, NFER.

Saury, J. & Durand, M. (1998). 'Practical knowledge in expert coaches: On-site study of coaching in sailing'. *Research Quarterly for Exercise and Sport,* 69 (3), pp. 254–266.

Schon, D.A. (1983). *The Reflective Practitioner: How Professionals Think in Action.* New York; Basic Books.

Walton, G. (1992). *Beyond Winning: The Timeless Wisdom of Great Philosopher Coaches.* Champaign, IL; Leisure Press.

Wildman, T. & Niles, J. (1987). 'Reflective teachers: Tensions between abstractions and realities'. *Journal of Teacher Education,* 38 (4), pp. 25–31.

chapter 6
knowledge for sports coaching

zoe avner

introduction

I spent three years at the French National Football Academy of Clairefontaine. Before entering the academy, I had gone through standard selection procedures including playing for my regional team, the Ile de France. My coach for the Ile de France team at the time was my future coach at the National Women's Football Academy. I will call him Alain for the purpose of this chapter. In total, Alain coached me for four years from the age of 16 to 20.

In this chapter, I plan to discuss an epiphanic moment or turning point in my football career that occurred while I was at the National Academy, concerning my relationship with my coach. This event had strong negative repercussions for me at the time and I still struggle with them to this day. Writing this chapter has helped me to see what influenced Alain's approach to coaching and made me see this painful event in a different light. Subsequently, I have been able to 're-conceptualise' this moment in my career in terms of a broader societal problem, rather than an individual failure. Therefore, this chapter is about how coaching must always be done with the understanding of the complexities of individual and cultural relationships.

At the National Academy, I was perceived as a shy, introverted girl, very different from the other girls who were loud and extrovert. Alain had a very definite idea about the different mental attributes that a high-level athlete needed to possess in order to achieve success; being shy and introverted did not fit into his ideal of a mentally strong athlete. It is precisely this concept of the mentally tough athlete that I plan to challenge in this chapter. To do so, I will first review a body of literature that might have informed Alain's idea of what attributes were required to be a mentally tough athlete and to succeed in high-level sport. I will then critique this first body of literature by introducing other texts such as Kenneth Gergen's (2000) *The Saturated Self,* which challenge this fixed ideal.

To shed light on this turning point in my life, I will refer to key ideas introduced by Gergen of the 'romanticist', 'modernist' and 'post-modernist' vision of the self. Since I will refer to these concepts throughout this chapter, I would first like to define what I mean by them in the next section of this chapter.

towards a fluid self

The values of the modernist paradigm and how it took over from a romantic paradigm are explained in Gergen's (2000) book *The Saturated Self,* the starting point for my reflection about identity and the practice of coaching. Gergen discusses the 'romanticist' view of the self as 'one that attributes to each person characteristics of personal depth: passion, soul, creativity, and moral fibre' (p. 6). He defines the 'modernist' view of the self in the following quote where he states that 'the chief characteristics of the self reside not in the domain of depth, but rather in our ability to reason in our beliefs, opinions, and conscious opinions' (p. 6). Finally, he combines the concept of the 'saturated self' with the post-modern era in which 'selves as possessors of real and identifiable characteristics, such as rationality, emotion, inspiration, and will are dismantled' and 'persons exist in a state of continuous construction and reconstruction' (p. 7). Now, to understand the context in which my epiphanic moment took place, I will next elaborate on my specific training environment and on my coach's personal background.

coaching football in france

Alain's education as a coach had followed a traditional path, acquiring all the different levels of French coaching certification before entering the Direction Technique Nationale, a very elitist and regulated coaching circle in which matters are dealt with in a certain way and no other. For example, there was a very strong sense of morality behind the idea of dealing with issues internally when it came to interpersonal conflict. There was also an unwritten rule of mutual support between the different coaches of the Direction Technique Nationale when it came to appointing a new coach for the national teams. This support and loyalty was apparent when a well-established member of the Direction Technique Nationale was appointed as the new French National Coach.

I believe Sage's (1989) concept of 'organisational socialisation' can help to illuminate this specific work subculture of the Direction Technique Nationale. Sage defines '"organisational socialisation" as the process by which "rookie coaches" on the job acquire the skills and supporting cultural ideology necessary to participate as contributing members of an occupation' (p. 87). As Sage emphasises in this particular passage, coaching practices are not born in a vacuum but are strongly influenced and shaped by the environment of learning and socialisation. Undoubtedly, Alain's coaching practice was strongly influenced by his learning environment within the Direction Technique Nationale.

However, it could also be argued that his approach to coaching and his image of the mentally tough player was also shaped by the traditional social values that his generation of coaches had grown up with and that were subsequently strongly reflected within the French National Coaching curriculum. Geoff Hare

(2003) articulates these traditional values when he talks about Aime Jacquet in his book about football in France:

> ⁶Having been mocked for his provincial accent and inarticulacy in front of the TV cameras, for his refusal to play the communication game and for generally being unfashionable, Jacquet now stood for virtues of hard work, modesty, humility, respect, honesty, rigour, simplicity, authenticity, competence, professionalism: all that was good in French tradition.⁹ (p. 116)

Aime Jacquet was Alain's mentor and his attachment to a romantic ideal of the French traditional values of post-war France was very much reflected in his coaching practice (*see* Hare, 2003). Liz Crolley & David Hand (2002) in their book *Football, Europe and the Press*, gathered a mass of data that corroborates the idea that specific socio-historical contexts can be directly related to specific ways of conceptualising the game, and of playing and coaching football in France. More notably, they discuss the impact of the industrial and the mining era and its subsequent decline on local people's attachment to certain values of courage, solidarity, hard work and resiliency. In the authors' terms, the local football players of these post-industrial depressed regions of France became iconic symbols of these idealised core regional values.

Alain was born and brought up in the Lorraine region, which had greatly suffered economically from the closing of the mining industry (Crolley & Hand, 2002, p. 79). Although I will never be able to assert that my coach's personal upbringing and background influenced the way he subsequently came to perceive his coaching role and shaped his idea about mental toughness, he nonetheless talked enough about his 'Lorraine natale' (native Lorraine) for me to be able to see that his specific socio-historical background could at least partially have shaped his views on mental toughness.

Alain had played good standard football in his Lorraine natale, where he had played for a division two team. However, he often referred to the frustration of his playing days as being linked to his role as a substitute. When he talked to me about his work, he described coaching in a very romantic way, using words such as 'true vocation', 'passion', 'sacrifice and total commitment' to describe his practice. Alain also used these romantic words to put down my club coach, who in his eyes didn't possess the attributes of good coaching since he lacked 'drive' and 'commitment'. It can be argued that Alain's frustration as a player made his drive to succeed as a coach all the more important. John Lyle (2002) in his book *Sports Coaching Concepts,* acknowledges in the following passage the intertwining and sometimes even competing influences that inform and shape the coaching practice:

❝ Despite the delivery and communication emphasis in the early stages of coach education, it seems unlikely that coach education is responsible for the development of coaching style. Many performance coaches rely heavily on their own experience as performers, and are recruited directly from active participation. ❞ (p. 163)

As Lyle claims, it would be reductive to consider that coaching courses and textbooks are the only sources that shape coaching practices and approaches. Clearly, one's own personal background and one's experience as a player are also very influential in determining the coach one will become. In this case, I believe that Alain's coaching style and his ideas about mental toughness were also strongly shaped by the type of coaching he had received and what had worked for him as a player.

Now that I have painted a general overview of the specific subculture of my training environment at the National Centre and seen the possible links that could be made between my coach's personal background and socialisation with his model of mental toughness, I will take a closer look at my coach's practice.

the practice of coaching

Alain's coaching practice could best be described as very thorough, logical and well structured. Our individual performances were rated quantitatively and we were regularly evaluated physically, technically, tactically and mentally. Alain's emphasis on a scientific approach to coaching is consistent with a modernist perspective, as described by Gergen (2000) in which he sees the modern era as one in which science and rationality prevail.

For the technical and physical aspects of the game we were evaluated through standardised tests to measure our progress. However, our tactical awareness and our mental qualities, were more of a personal subjective judgement based on Alain's observations, since these skills are difficult to quantify scientifically. The difficulty of assessing and evaluating players' tactical awareness and, even more so, players' psychological attributes stems from two structural problems. The first is the lack of a clearly defined and consensual conceptual framework consisting of the psychological attributes necessary for young athletes aspiring to reach the highest level in their specific sport. The second problem is linked to the absence of a consensual and clear methodology as to how to identify and test for these desirable psychological attributes (Morris, 2000, p. 722).

Alain also placed a strong emphasis on the idea of professionalism. In retrospect, the fact that he would continuously refer to himself as a 'professional' came to mean to me that he was 100 per cent objective and infallible. I believe that Michel Foucault's idea of 'discourses' can help to illuminate why I associated the idea of professionalism with objectivity and truth. Foucault defines discourses as 'a group of statements which provide a language for talking about – a way of representing knowledge about – a particular topic at a particular historical moment' (from Hall, 1997, p. 44). Foucault's idea is that discourses provide the language available to us to express concepts such as professionalism. However, by giving us the language to discuss these ideas, discourses simultaneously restrict and constrain our thoughts and subsequently our actions. In Foucault's terms, discourses create knowledge and truth, which in turn create power and vice versa in an everlasting cycle. Therefore, this discourse of professionalism empowered Alain by legitimising his knowledge and his claims to truth, which subsequently led us to believe that every action he took and word he said was conscious, balanced and deliberate and therefore could not be questioned or dismissed as irrational. This robotic, machine-like conception of the human mind and body is also characteristic of a modernist view of the self. And this metaphor of the human mind as a machine is important because it strengthened the dichotomy between Alain the person and Alain the coach. It also served to reinforce his claim that it is possible to successfully switch in and out of each role when appropriate. More importantly, by adopting this scientific, professional approach to coaching, it made it very difficult for us as players to question his ideas and decisions as a coach. Therefore, I logically accepted his mental model of the mental attributes of a high-profile athlete as scientifically sound and unquestionable.

a model of mental toughness

In Alain's mental model of the high-performance athlete, an extremely high degree of resilience, dedication, concentration, motivation and, above all, self-confidence, were seen as indispensable attributes of the mentally tough athlete. Patricia Miller & Gretchen Kerr (2002) in their essay 'Conceptualising Excellence: Past, Present and Future', distinguish between four different periods in sport psychology. The earliest period places great emphasis on performance excellence and on 'identifying personality profiles that would distinguish exceptional athletes and permit predictions of athletic success based on various personality traits' (p. 142).

Alain's model of the mentally tough athlete coincides with this early philosophy and approach in sport psychology, prominent in the 1960s. Early sport psychological research came up with the following specific traits and profiles in their talent identification: 'research consistently suggested the "iceberg profile" marked by low scores on the tension, depression, anger, fatigue and confusion scales and a high score on the vigour scale of the Profile of Mood States and distinguished skilled from lesser skilled athletes' (Miller & Kerr, 2002, p. 142). This model of mental toughness continues to be influential even in recent research. In their article that seeks to define and understand mental toughness in soccer, Richard Thelwell, Neil Weston and Iain Greenlees (2005) were able to draw on a recent body of research that suggests, 'that mentally tough performers hold several key attributes, which enable them to experience positive psychological states'. Examples of these include 'commitment and determination, motivation and control, excellent concentration and focusing abilities and confidence and self-belief' (p. 326). A noteworthy point is that the attributes of this 'iceberg profile' are thought to be inborn and inherent to the self. In other words, this higher mental talent is inherited, present within the self and cannot be learnt. This might explain why Alain never developed a strategy to develop this desired mental toughness and concentrated all his efforts on developing technical expertise. Although, another plausible explanation would be that he simply didn't know how to help us acquire these mental skills. Whether he didn't believe we could develop these mental skills or whether he didn't know how to teach this mental attitude, it nevertheless left me feeling helpless. On the one hand, I was labelled as 'faulty' because I was considered as lacking self-confidence and self-assertiveness and on the other, I wasn't given the tools to improve or, maybe more importantly, I wasn't led to believe that I could improve. In these circumstances this specific model of mental toughness in sport was extremely destructive because not only did I fail to reach the standards of mental toughness required at the time, but it was also implied that I would never be able to reach them.

Alain's discourse about mental toughness was also problematic because it locked my relationship with him into certain specific patterns. I never felt that I could have genuine conversations with him and talk to him openly about problems that I was having, such as coping with injuries or with his particular style of coaching. This mental toughness model made me believe that something was wrong with me and that I was weak because my body kept breaking down and because I didn't cope very well emotionally with his style of coaching. This model also led me to do things that were detrimental to my health. An example of this is the way I chose to continue to train for a whole week with a pulled hamstring because I had already been injured that month and I didn't want Alain to think that I was weak or that I was trying to get out of training. Ultimately, this mental toughness discourse reinforced my feeling that I didn't have the mental makeup to play at the highest level. It might very well be that if I had felt that I could have expressed my discomfort at the time, I would have met a positive and constructive response in return. However, since I didn't feel that I could voice my problems, my coach and I were stuck in a fake and superficial relationship that was not beneficial to my development as a player.

an epiphanic moment in my football career

Although my coach made frequent references to this mental model of toughness, he had never targeted me directly in public. This was to change when our academy played the French National Team. Although the game was just a friendly, it was nonetheless a massive game for us girls at the academy as it was a rare opportunity for us to impress the head coach of the national team who was in the process of selecting a squad for the upcoming European Championship. We were all really nervous and anxious to do well and Alain didn't calm our nerves when he came out with the following words: 'Girls, this is a massive game for us, if we play well today it will mean that the philosophy that we have developed here is the right one and the head coach of the French national team will have to reconsider the squad she selected'. Unfortunately, the game didn't go that well for our academy and we lost 2–0. I also personally didn't put in a great display and I was feeling really frustrated and disappointed after the game.

As a general rule, the whole squad would sit down for a short post-game debriefing with our coach. That day was no exception and our coach had some pretty hard words for us. He told us that we had put in a particularly poor performance and that this suggested to him that we were not at all ready to contend for a spot on the national team. In that post-game debriefing, he also singled me out by saying, 'Zoe, shyness is a weakness and there is no room for shy people in high-performance sport. I would much rather have an overly confident player'. Those words stung, not only because he had said them publicly and in front of the national team coach, but also because they epitomised my feeling of inadequacy. This feeling had been growing steadily and that particular post-game debriefing acted as a kind of trigger for me. I left that meeting with a new and strong feeling that I quite simply lacked the necessary mental makeup for this level of competition and that I might as well give up on my aspirations since I was never going to be able to change.

This idea of change in self-identity is quite interesting because I wrestled with it in numerous ways. First, I found it extremely difficult to change other people's perceptions of me. On the few occasions where I deliberately acted out of character, motivated by the desire to change my coach's and my team-mates perception of me as a shy, introverted girl, my efforts backfired and I was sanctioned. Also, my own romantic vision of the self and identity implied a certain cohesion and logic between who I was on the pitch and who I was in other parts of my life. Therefore, I almost felt that I was cheating on myself when I attempted to be loud and extroverted. I suppose that in this respect I was very much influenced by a romantic vision of the self in which one's identity is fixed, inborn and consistent (*see* Gergen, 2000, p. 19). As a result, my attempts to adopt Alain's model of mental toughness felt like a treachery to my authentic and moral self. I felt strongly that this authentic self was not compatible with my

that psychological characteristics remain stable from adolescence to adulthood in the context of elite sport' (p. 717) . . . (not my own words). The idea that psychological traits in an individual can evolve and that they are actually highly likely to evolve in the context of sport supports Morris's recommendation for coaches and sport psychologists to focus on the field of psychological skill training. He claims that the 'use of resources in the development of goal setting, anxiety management, concentration and confidence-building skills in many junior players has the potential to enhance their ability to cope with the increasing demands of the elite adult game and to promote their continued enjoyment of the game' (Morris, 2000, p. 723).

However, in light of Foucault's discussion about knowledge and power, Morris's strategy could be seen as equally problematic. Indeed, Morris (2000) advocates the development of 'coping skills' for athletes of the elite game. By doing this, he focuses on helping athletes cope with the increasing demands of high-performance sport, but fails to draw attention to larger issues and conflicts of interest that are produced by certain discourses in sport. The idea that useful mental skills can be taught just like technical prowess is a reassuring and engaging idea. However, it doesn't challenge the dominant discourse about mental toughness that was problematic for me. Instead, it continues to take an athlete-centred approach focused on changing the individual athlete to fit some standard of 'mental toughness'.

Although Thelwell et al. (2005) in their essay 'Defining mental toughness within soccer' draw a restrictive and restricted model for mental toughness, they do nonetheless acknowledge, 'there is a requirement to examine alternative perceptions to the mentally tough player' (p. 332). This recommendation is consistent with a trend to look at alternative ways of conceptualising sport, sport excellence and sport ethics. Patricia Miller & Gretchen Kerr (2002) in 'Conceptualising excellence: Past, present, and future' warn of the dangers of focusing solely on sport excellence. One of these is the danger of early identity foreclosure that leads to dependence and poor moral development. The authors define 'early identity foreclosure' as a state in which individuals limit themselves to a conferred role identity, fail to reflect on whether this conferred role identity matches their potentially evolving worldview and personal ambitions and, finally, limit planning and investment in future selves. To counter these negative outcomes, Miller and Kerr (2002) advocate a better balance between sport excellence and personal excellence and encourage people working in the field of sport to develop a sport environment in which performance and personal excellence are equally valued. They go so far as to suggest, 'performance excellence is attained only through optimal personal development' (p. 141).

This is an interesting point of view when I relate it to my experience. Indeed, Miller & Gretchen's (2002) idea of 'personal' and 'performance selves' being equally valued and developed in concordance goes against my personal experience of the 'performing self' being developed at the expense of the 'personal self' and vice versa.

If I had trained in the ideal environment that the authors describe, then maybe I would not have experienced this feeling of fragmentation and dislocation of the self quite as strongly.

Shogan, in her book *The Making of the High-performance Athlete: Discipline, Diversity and Ethics* (1999), also points out the need to look at new ways of conceptualising behaviour in sport. She argues for promoting hybridity and diversity in sport as a way to counter potentially abusive sport disciplines. She claims that: 'the hybridity and diversity of participants guarantee that no one participates in high-performance sport in the same way and that no one is ever consumed by sport discipline' (p. 101). By sport discipline, Shogan means both discipline as the body of knowledge of sport, and also discipline as control 'such that the body of knowledge that constitutes the "discipline" of high-performance sport is knowledge of the technologies that 'discipline' or control athletic bodies' (p. 10).

However, Shogan (1999) takes her reflection one step further. She actually promotes hybridity and diversity as a strategy, not only to counter the abuses of sport discipline, but also to challenge the status quo resulting from powerful hegemonic discourses. She believes that hybridity and diversity will help to uncover dissonances and conflicts of interest between disciplines. Noticing these disruptions will, according to Shogan, 'create the possibility of new ways of understanding and participating in high-performance sport' (p. 101). This is an interesting point because it goes totally against my personal experience at the

National Academy. Indeed, there was no room for diversity and hybridity in my training environment as we were supposed to be 'moulded' into footballers according to certain well-established standards of excellence. I was so physically and mentally immersed in this specific training culture and structure that I was unable to conceive of any alternative ways to participate in high-performance athletics.

This leads to my final thought about the ways in which a sport discipline can be abusive. Indeed, the mental model of the tough athlete that I bought into implied a very high degree of commitment and dedication to succeed. Though a high degree of commitment and dedication are clearly important in high-level sport, as this chapter has suggested, these concepts need to be handled carefully and critically, especially by the coach. One needs to understand that these terms are powerful, potentially dangerous and problematic. Although, it was not always clearly stated, it was generally implied by Alain that we should eat, breathe and sleep football and there was therefore very little time for different experiences. Even when I did have the opportunity to go out and socialise with non-football crowds, I tended to restrict myself because potentially I thought it might hinder my sporting performance. As a consequence, I now realise that I very much developed a one-dimensional identity that revolved around football and that I was therefore much more susceptible to suffer and to struggle with failure to reach my athletic goals. What I contest, in light of Foucault's work, is not that dedication, commitment and such qualities are unimportant in sport. Rather, I contest that complying with this specific socio-historical discourse of mental toughness is the only way to participate and to be successful in high-performance sport.

conclusion

In conclusion, I would say that there is the need to challenge the early but nonetheless influential model of mental toughness that influenced my coach. Therefore, coaches need to start thinking about these influential ideas, not as universal and fixed truths, but as versions of the truth amongst many others that have simply been pushed to the top of the hierarchy of ideas by certain mechanisms linked to power and knowledge. By starting to think of these mental models as influential ideas instead of scientific truths one might open up, as Shogan (1999) points out, new ways of understanding and engaging in high-performance sport (p. 101). Finally, I end by quoting Foucault as he advocates for a 'hyper and pessimistic activism' that I believe can be useful for every coach to keep in mind as they develop their coaching identity and philosophy:

'I am not looking for an alternative . . . you see, what I want to do is not the history of solutions, and that's the reason why I don't accept the word 'alternative'. I would like to do genealogy of problems, of *problematiques*. My point is not that everything is bad but that everything is dangerous, which is not exactly the same as bad. If everything is dangerous, then we always have something to do. So my position leads not to apathy but to a hyper- and pessimistic activism. ' (Gutting, 1994, p. 112.)

references

Crolley, L. & Hand, D. (2002). *Football, Europe and the Press*. London; Frank Cass Publishers.

Gergen, K.J. (2000). *The Saturated Self*. New York; Basic Books.

Gutting, G. (1994). *The Cambridge Companion to Foucault*. Cambridge; Cambridge University Press.

Hall, S. (1997). *Representation*. London; Sage.

Hare, G. (2003). *Football in France: A Cultural History*. New York; Berg.

Jones, R.L., Armour, K.M. & Potrac, P. (2002). 'Understanding the coaching process: A framework for social analysis'. *Quest*, 2002, 54, pp. 34–48.

Lyle, J. (2002). *Sports Coaching Concepts: A Framework for Coaches' Behaviour*. London; Routledge.

Miller, P.S. & Kerr, G.A. (2002). 'Conceptualizing Excellence: Past, Present, and Future'. *Journal of Applied Sport Psychology*, 14, pp. 140–153.

Morris, T. (2000). 'Psychological characteristics and talent identification in soccer'. *Journal of Sports Sciences*, 18, pp. 715–726.

Sage, G. (1989). 'Becoming a high school coach: From playing sport to coaching'. *Research Quarterly for Exercise and Sport*, 60 (1), pp. 81–92.

Shogan, D. (1999). *High Performance Athletes, Discipline, Diversity and Ethics*. Buffalo, Canada; University of Toronto Press.

Thelwell, R., Weston, N. & Greenlees, I. (2005). 'Defining and Understanding Mental Toughness within Soccer'. *Journal of Applied Sport Psychology*, 17, pp. 326–332.

Vealey (1992). In Morris, T. 'Psychological characteristics and talent identification in soccer'. *Journal of Sports Sciences*, 18, pp. 715–726.

part 3
the coaching act
norman, hardes, jones

chapter 7
coach interview: lyn gunson

leanne norman

introduction

Much has been written about women in sport, with a great deal of research devoted to understanding women's sporting experiences. Statistics detailing participation rates in sport and physical activity in the UK demonstrate a dramatic increase in the number of women taking part in a variety of sports, showing women now enjoy higher participation rates than ever before. The social and cultural perceptions of women are also changing along with increasing opportunities for women in sport. Much of this advancement can be accredited to the impact of the feminist movement that has grown to prominence since the 1970s, which has deliberately placed the concern of social change for women at the heart of theoretical development and research activity. The goal of feminist theory is to end the social oppression of women. However, for this to be realised, there is a great deal more to be learned. While there is an abundant body of research literature concerning women's and girl's sporting experiences, very little is known about women in powerful and senior positions of coaching and leadership in sport. With a paucity of women in such positions, it is an area that has not been granted the in-depth attention it deserves.

In this chapter I present an interview with Lyn Gunson, Director of Netball for TeamBath and Director of Athletic Development for England Under-21 Netball. This interview, which is grounded in a feminist cultural studies conceptual framework, seeks to elicit Lyn's experiences as an elite woman coach and to contribute to an understanding of the complexities and challenges women coaches face, how women leaders are received in such a male dominated profession and culture, as well as how women coaches have negotiated social expectations and cultural norms to reach their position. This interview documents how Lyn has negotiated and managed her career path, how she has experienced gender relations in sport as well as her ideas for empowering and increasing women's political voice and power in sport.

Leanne Norman: Could you tell me about your journey up the coaching ladder and how you became interested in coaching?

Lyn Gunson: I guess it depends on what you define as coaching, because I feel as though I have been coaching all my life. Even at high school I was coaching other kids all the time and in lots of different sports. I probably began coaching in a formal sense when I was about 13 or 14. And then when I went through high school and went to university, again it was the same thing. It was a provincial side, which was in the first division in the top competition in New Zealand, and I ended up player-coach which was very unusual and it was the first time that anyone had done that in New Zealand. The players actually coached, and I was the captain, so I became pretty much the coach and after the second year I was basically coaching that provincial side. From then on I was just coaching no matter what. I have just gone through coaching provincial sides and I have coached New Zealand and England and age-group sides. I have had a lot to do with national development to where I am now, currently involved in coach education as well as coaching the under-21 side. One of my main roles at the moment is as performance coach for England Netball, but the actual formal thing I do is coach the under-21 team.

LN: So, you say getting into coaching was quite circumstantial, what were your other reasons?

LG: Some of it was [circumstantial], but just really a desire to help other people because I didn't find it difficult to play sport and I didn't find it difficult to understand what was going on. So it wasn't that much of a step to take up a leadership type role.

LN: You have obviously reached the top of the coaching ladder; have you found the progression quite smooth? Have you always wanted to reach the top?

LG: I never sat down and saw it in a career pathway type way. I have just moved along and coached, which has seemed the sensible thing to do. I enjoy challenges; I like problem solving and working out difficult things. I have done quite a bit of coaching in other countries as well. And I think probably I get asked to do that because I have a reasonable background in being very accepting of lots of different coaches and don't seem to have a problem with getting on with people in different environments. So I've coached in Jamaica and South Africa.

LN: During the early stages of your coaching career, would you say you had any role models or mentors?

LG: Yes, my mother. My mother was an independent, spirited person with a lot of energy. She didn't let things get in her way if she wanted to do something. I guess that independence of spirit is probably something I've lived with: you just get on with it in the belief that you can do things. That attitude does come from people around you. In New Zealand, in our district, we were all like that, all the women. They didn't sit down and moan about their problems, they just got up and did something about it. You know, resourceful, self-sufficient. And probably that's happened here at Bath. The English girls were really different for me to deal with when I came. They were culturally very different. It was very difficult for them because at the start you had to teach a whole new way of looking at it. Not just netball, but life generally. We had situations in the sports hall where the guys would just walk through our training area and that sort of thing. I had a lot of trouble getting them into the weights area. We had to talk a lot about gender and not taking this abuse as we have the right because we're women; my attitude was not about that. You need to do this, because as a person, you have the right to do this not just as a male or female. So, in that way, I was teaching them some independence they wouldn't have had.

LN: You were saying you had difficulties getting the players into the strength and conditioning room, what do you mean by that?

LG: There are difficulties with body image perceptions, there's all sorts of cultural issues about how they [the netballers] perceive what that will mean and how other people will perceive them. They get put into some boxes really. I've taught them not to react to that but to stand up for themselves. There are other coaches in here – male coaches – who, at the start, were saying things like, 'What are you doing in here, you have got no muscle definition and your sport is just a throwaway, so what the heck are you guys doing in here?' They would just leave huge weights on the bars so the girls would have to go and ask one of the guys to shift the big weights. They hang around and they crowd the space. After about a week I got sick of it. And so I said to the players, 'Do you think this is OK? You know, these guys walking through your training session?' They asked, 'What can we do about it?' So I said that I was not going to put up with it any longer. So I went the next week and said very politely, 'Excuse me, can you go around?' and they completely ignored me. So I just stepped in front and said, 'I'm very sorry but I mean this, I would like you to go around the court, there is a safety reason'. They couldn't believe I had tackled these people. So then they cottoned on to it and they started to do things to establish their space. You have to draw lines on behaviour, but I've always believed that your value basis is what drives that. And my value basis has always been about fairness, about being courteous, and about being kind and helpful to people. Not just about the sport's values: it's about much more than that. But I don't go off into any other political values either; for me it's more of a fundamental human dignity thing. And I've found that usually works best.

LN: In what ways have you had support and guidance from other women coaches?

LG: Almost none. I probably haven't had much guidance from anybody. But I've learned a lot myself, as I'm quite self-reflective.

LN: Why do you think you haven't had much support from other women coaches?

LG: There are not that many around. There is certainly one woman that's been helpful to me at Bath; in the sense it's been helpful to be able to talk to somebody about issues on the same level. She's very articulate, very intelligent and a very capable person. There's another person I know who is very sensitive emotionally, and another one who is very pragmatic and straight to the point. The people I deal with the most, they probably do give me that support. That way, I think you naturally seek out the people who are going to help you, but it won't necessarily be about the game.

LN: In your role as a senior coach, as director of netball for TeamBath and your position in the England netball set-up, could you describe your daily routine? How do you plan and manage your responsibilities each day?

LG: I'm responsible for an international situation in which we're doing an assessment with the African nations for what they need to do to improve. So that's one. The second thread is national material, which means I have to help all the national coaches in the Superleague – I'm primarily responsible for the south-west group. I have about 15 coaches I have to deal with regularly. The other national role that goes on alongside that is the under-21 programme which I'm now setting up for the next three years. And then there's a regional role, which is this university and its relationship to the region, and the Superleague. And then the fourth one is actually on-site with the university club. At the moment I'm the only person doing all of it. And it's a lot of work. So, my day has been like this generally: a seven-day week usually from September to December and then from January to May. During the week in the morning, it's 7am training because the group here on-site needs help. And then each night there is either elite training or something else in between, the players come in and then there's a lot of pastoral care to do. So the day will be from 7am through to probably 9pm. While Superleague is finishing, I'm already planning the beginning of next season. So there are several parts of me operating at the same time. The reason we survive like this is simply because what I've done with the players is to try and make them self-sufficient. So I'm trying to get them to go away from this place to be independent women who can control their lives and get on with it. But they need to take responsibility for what's happening to them.

LN: So the many roles you have appear to be very demanding.

LG: Yes, but some of them are exciting because they're real challenges. But if you stop to think about it, like if you go to South Africa, which we did a couple of months ago for a week, as well

as present a report to the government, the roles are quite responsible as well. People want to use netball as a tool because they
want women to develop and it's a relatively non-threatening
environment. We've been to some meetings where men were
involved and the men were very harsh on the women in those
meetings. In fact, in one meeting they also scorned them enough
not to say anything. The game of netball has always been able to
be more than a game. It's more of a life development situation
for women.

**LN: Have you experienced any differences in how you have
been perceived as a coach in different cultures?**

LG: Oh, absolutely. But that happens even within the same culture,
and in different areas within the country. And also with players
who have different experiences in sport. I can always tell when
they come from a sport which is dominated by male coaches.

LN: How so?

LG: There is a tendency for a lot of men coaches to be autocratic. So the women in netball, if they've been in other sports,
are used to quite controlling behaviour. It is coach-led rather
than player-centred. People wait to be told what to do and they
don't show much initiative; they don't show as much decision
making, and are reliant on external motivations and external

rewards. In a way, I'm known as coaching in a slightly different way from that.

LN: In what way would you say you are different?

LG: I don't believe that women in sport, and this is a generalisation, analyse that well. They tend to be very emotive in the way they receive information. I coach in a much more direct, honest way in terms of what's happening and how the athlete perceives that. On the other hand, I'm not like a lot of the guys because I tend not to be autocratic; I want the player to do things for herself.

LN: Would you say you have adapted your coaching style in any way from a traditional style to what it is now?

LG: I wouldn't say I've changed my coaching style. I have always been like that. I still think it comes from a fundamental desire to help people, because I don't see myself as a person who knows everything or the person who they [the athletes] should rely on. I would like athletes to be more self-reliant and, if they are, they have a better capacity to achieve and reach their potential because they explore and attack problems rather than being determined by what other people tell them. So that puts the coach in a secondary role in the sense that the athlete is at the centre of it, rather than, I think a lot of coaches try and own the player's development and performance. And I don't believe that's the best thing to do, so you come up with strategies and ways to try and create conditions by which the athlete can develop their own performance and feel ownership of it.

LN: How have your players responded to that style of coaching?

LG: It's quite a shock to them at the start because you are very blunt, you know, this is what has happened, now we need to fix it. Or 'What do you think is happening?' I do a lot of asking questions and they are very direct and pointed towards perform-ance. And most women, they don't cut with that very well at the start because they internalise that and they take it on emotion-ally, rather than just as factual information. They struggle with it, so it takes quite a while to get to a point where they can sit down and talk about their performance in an unemotional way. For example, 'I was good at this, but I need to do this, this and this'.

LN: We are starting to touch upon barriers and challenges that women coaches have to face. Have you experienced any obstacles or barriers in your development as a coach?

LG: I don't think I have. I just feel I've had to work harder sometimes. Although I do find I have to be more assertive, and as a person I actually struggle with that because I'm quite shy and quiet. So when I'm in this kind of environment, I find it's a bit stressful in the sense I feel like I'm not the person I really am. It could be that I'm not the right *looking* kind of woman because I think there are some women have particular facial features in some cultures that will get things easier than the others of us who don't look like that. It would be easier, I'm not saying much easier, but it definitely would be easier.

LN: Do you think women coaches offer anything that's special or different? Some people argue that a coach's sex is irrelevant as long as they are effective.

LG: If women use a bit of the emotional material better they would contribute that. But I really don't feel sex has been an issue in lots of ways. There are so many other factors that are intertwined with coaching. To be honest, I don't really think of it as 'us and them', you know, males and females. I just think about people.

LN: Why don't you think there are more senior women coaches in sport?

LG: I think most women prefer to do other things and I don't think women like the accountability that goes with coaching at the highest level. It's a bit like men who've got the responsibility of their families, like the feeling you're responsible for your family's welfare and getting money for that. If you're in coaching, you're constantly under pressure to perform and I personally don't think a lot of women like that. Particularly if they've been in the home, they're used to a different kind of pressure. It's not public, it's a juggling pressure of lots of activities happening and kids going here, them trying to work and juggle that. It's a balancing act rather than a direct 'here's the pressure, here's the result, and here's the accountability structure'.

LN: In what ways do you think women possess influence and control in your sport?

LG: In netball women do hold powerful positions. But I have found that the coach is at the bottom of those power positions. Instead, the administrators are very powerful. In England Netball, the people with the information are actually the coaches, but the administrators are actually making decisions without even talking to coaches about serious things like the Superleague and how it should proceed. What I find with coaching generally is that the coach is often the last one that's actually talked to. Supposedly, everything is athlete-centred but it seems to me that the coaches more often than not have something they can add.

LN: In what ways do you think men possess influence and control in your sport?

LG: Well, how the women are operating at the moment is 'round the back', very little honesty up front and lots of manipulation behind the scenes. Men seem to be able to have a bust up and for it to be OK the next day. That's not my experience of women or some sections of women. It's not a nice characteristic to work with because the rules are changing all the time. It makes the profession look less effective and much more problematic, more tedious and more emotionally draining because of how they operate. In netball women occupy pretty much all of the positions. Except, very often the finance person is a male. And there are men coaches in netball. You see, this is what's interesting. There are few women coaches but in netball, most of the coaches are women. So why is that? What it is about that environment that they're OK with that they're not OK with in the co-ed sports?

LN: What are the reactions to men who coach netball?

LG: Women receive them [men coaches] very well. There are men that come in as support staff in some other countries; they have a real problem with this. In some countries, transvestites or gay guys are actually using women because they feel safe in netball. So they tend to migrate towards it, and in some countries, they have almost no women coaches anymore because these men have moved in on coaching and they also pick it up as a career opportunity. It looks as though women don't see coaching as a career opportunity or a career path. Partly because it's not very obvious, but also in a lot of the women sports, there are not full-time jobs or anything anyway. So they tend to go for safe occupations.

LN: In such a male-dominated environment, have you witnessed different coaching styles of men and women? You mentioned that women operate in a more emotional manner compared to men.

LG: Well, I don't think it is a gender thing because I have seen a whole lot of women coaches that are autocratic. Now I think that's because they have come through a system that has taught them that's how they should coach. So what you've got is a system of sport which is quite determined by men, then it infiltrates how everyone gets taught to coach. So the women are just as autocratic as some of the guys. By that I mean they are very dominant and they tell people what to do, they demand certain formations and the way in which decisions are constructed, the athlete then starts to become dependent upon them. So I'm not convinced it's a gender thing in the sense that women are this and men are that. But I've seen the whole situation create women coaches that are the same type of coaches as men because they've come through that whole structure.

LN: Do you think that is cross-cultural?

LG: Yes I do. Some cultures, like the Pacific Oceans group for example, the men, if you listen to them, sound very bossy. Sometimes I have had to adapt; if I have had difficulty explaining something to a player in netball, then I have looked at what culture they have come from and I've adapted some language sometimes to make the point. So someone who is used to that very bossy, male-dominant behaviour, and if it's how the women are in the family as well, sometimes the players then need you to be very direct and blunt in the way they're used to receiving information. I have seen women in netball then have difficulties at home because they have become more independent, they have become self-reliant, they have become more confident in who they are. For some of them, relationship-wise, it causes problems. In netball a lot of females play it and so women have been able to have an atmosphere which is different than if men were involved. So sometimes they grow in a way they wouldn't have if both sexes had been involved.

LN: How do you feel the media perceive women in sport in general, with sport being such a visible part of culture?

LG: Well, it's not for women. I mean, it's visible for men. The first problem you have got with netball in England is that it's invisible. So for a start, kids learn visually. So the women coaches have got a problem for a start because they haven't got anything visual to say, 'Look, this is what it should look like'. Even within New Zealand, you know, it's only 6 per cent of resources [that] go towards women's activity. It's not just because people see it, it is how it's portrayed. Like if you listen to commentators for sport, you can hear the way in which men say things and how they talk about women's sport. I think men view women's sport as superimposed: as what they are normally used to looking at [in men's sport], they then use to look at women's sport. So you have to actually teach or encourage people to look at different characteristics and value them. Why don't people want to watch the women as much, and why don't they get paid as much money? Now my question is: is it promoted in the way that people can learn to watch it in a positive way? And I don't think it is. I think it's the values placed on to it or the way they superimpose a lot. Now, what breaks that up, of course, are people like the Williams' sisters in tennis who come along and start playing like the men. So straight away, people start watching women's sport. Then you may get another female come along, like Chris Everett, and so you go back to a different style and so people go off it again. A different style of woman comes in and all of a sudden, people are more interested in watching.

LN: What impact do you think that has on women, to be seen in those ways?

LG: Well, in some ways, they want notoriety but they don't want what goes with it. So I think they get mad that they are not as well known or don't get as much support as the men.

I mean, that certainly happens here; the players get frustrated with the amount of support some groups get when they don't perform at the level that they do. But there is this perception that netball is a throw-away sport.

LN: How have you, if at all, experienced any personal conflict between being a woman and a sportswoman?

LG: Yes I can imagine that. I mean, with the players, as soon as they became more assertive, the guys tended to just 'pigeon-hole' them into being either non-feminine or a lesbian. You could see they were very conscious of not being 'pigeon-holed'. But some of them I've seen, in their relationships, have also had trouble. So, if they've had a boyfriend, that guy has had to learn to cope with this new person and in a couple of cases they haven't been able to.

LN: What do you think has been the initial reaction to feeling they are being 'pigeon-holed'?

LG: They lose confidence straight away and then they start to see there's another world that they can look at as well. It's not taking anything away; it's about who you can be if you really want to.

LN: Have you experienced any of that 'pigeon-holing' yourself?

LG: Yes, so much so that if someone comes to our house and sees me cooking, they just can't get over that. That's not the image of what a sportswoman should be doing. I like reading and all sorts of things; the guys get a real surprise. They become very accepting but at the start, they would get a real surprise if I went to the theatre. I think that's the problem with sportspeople, the sport itself almost debilitates them to explore other parts of themselves. They get to a point where they don't feed their growth and development as a person.

LN: You mentioned earlier using netball as a tool. Do you think sport is a suitable or significant vehicle to empower women?

LG: Netball can do so because essentially it is women playing. I'm not sure about other sports.

LN: You also mentioned women possessing power in various cultures; do you think that if women had more power in sport, in terms of senior positions or a political voice, that would impact upon women in general?

LG: No, I don't actually. The reason I say that is most of the women I have seen get into powerful positions actually get colonised by the power. They end up behaving like the men do.

And I've seen it happen a lot, whereas the men will work on networks, women tend to hold grudges for a long period of time. Women who get through in companies, not just sport, they don't help women at all. I would rather go and ask a man for sponsorship than a woman. In some ways, it's almost like payback, you know, 'I've got through this system and you will have to do it the hard way'. But my own personal experience has shown me that women don't necessarily help other women.

LN: How do you think we could get more women into senior coaching positions?

LG: Well, we're dealing with these performance coaches. They're really quite scared of the responsibility. I think you have to nurture younger coaches and give them the environment that helps them grow better or help them grow better until they're confident enough to step forward into that environment. We've protected them and got them into an environment where we've said making mistakes is fine, no one is going to jump on you. They've been quite cooperative, but they are going to get to the point where they're going to get competitive because they want to go for the same jobs. That needs managing as well, but the point is they are getting there and they want to do it. It is about seeing it as a career, because it's quite demanding time-wise.

LN: Do you consider the work that you are involved in with the performance coaches to be successful?

LG: Well, this is the second year of the programme. Yes, I think we are making a difference but then we've done it in a completely different way. It's completely experience and totally coach-centred. And there is no hierarchy of development; it's more like a jigsaw. What do people need, what do they perceive their needs are now, what do they need to do, how can we do this in such a way that has an impact on them? Let's do real-time stuff and so real things. It's not like some of them are simulated, that's not as real as you can get.

LN: How have the coaches themselves experienced the programme?

LG: They love it and everyone is fighting to get on the programme. It is definitely giving these women confidence. We've put them in that environment at the start, they've come through, gained some confidence and they're really starting to take on board what they need to do.

chapter 8
coach interview:
chris volley

jennifer hardes

introduction

The complex transition from athlete to coach is the narrative to unfold from Chris Volley, the lead Triathlon Coach at the University of Bath's High Performance Centre. Volley has been managing the triathlon programme at Bath since October 2005, after refocusing his efforts as an elite triathlete. The following chapter examines his professional coaching practice and his understanding of coaching in a results-driven climate. Volley shares his experiences that have shaped his own coaching knowledge, and his integrity about his coaching values is creditable and provides an insight into future coaching pathways.

Jennifer Hardes: Hi, Chris. Can we start by discussing your experiences of coaching triathlon here at the University of Bath, your role and how you've found it so far?

Chris Volley: I coach both the elite performers here at Bath and recreational triathlon so I've taken on a spectrum of coaching roles. I deal with elites in terms of the TeamBath programme and the World Class programme, but I also have a role as the Student Triathlon Club Coach. That's literally for people who are interested in triathlon and want to have a go.

JH: How long have you been coaching here?

CV: I've been in the job approximately one year. The job I've taken on has changed quite a lot from what was the original structure. It's essentially gone from three coaches down to myself and all of the three coaches who were here previously had nothing to do with the centre, so it's been a steep learning curve. I've had to put together my own programme based around my own philosophies and it's been a real challenge. It's nice to have a blank canvas, but it's also been tough, when you're not as experienced as maybe I should be, to come in and set up your own structure.

JH: Do you think having a blank canvas and being a relatively novice coach has had a positive influence on your transition

from being an athlete yourself, or might it have been easier had you been more experienced?

CV: I do think I'm really lucky because there are very few coaches who have that opportunity, in a centre like this with the facilities and obviously the raw materials in terms of athletes, to just be told to do what you want to do. So it was daunting being a novice, but it's given me freedom to take it forward in the direction I would like. I'm in a strange situation in that I was a member of the triathlon group, and a fairly established member of that group, so for me to then have to almost sit outside the circle and become the coach was a slightly daunting move. I think I was fortunate that I was an experienced member of the group and so I probably partly played a coaching role anyway, and was labelled a coach. Therefore, it's not too bad that I've stepped up and most of the people have accepted that role change.

JH: Would you say that it has had a constructive impact on your athletes in terms of them having previously known you as a performer?

CV: On the whole I think it's been good and it's made it slightly easier, but I do see its limitations. People know my strengths and weaknesses, as in personality, and they can exploit those if they want. Rather than me coming in with a clean slate and saying 'This is how it is, this is how I want things to be done, and this is why'; on the other hand I haven't necessarily had to earn the athletes' trust, but I have had to earn their respect as a coach rather than just another athlete.

JH: Within coaching there appears to be a shift from the traditional authoritative coaching role to hearing terms such as 'athlete empowerment' and 'shared responsibility' so perhaps you could say that less of an authoritative role isn't necessarily problematic?

CV: Whether coaches need that hierarchical role or not would depend on the situation they are in: be it the age, experience of athletes, and the age and experience of the coach. I have definitely gone down the way of being a coach who likes to encourage athlete empowerment. I think when I was doing my coaching degree it was something which really struck a chord with me. It does have its limitations and it is tough at times, but that's the way I am as a person and I think I'm just letting that come through. I try not to be a different person when I've got my coaching hat on to when I'm outside the centre, and I think it would have looked very false had I suddenly been given the coaching badge and just jumped straight into an authoritative role. The process I've taken from the start was to try to get athletes to take responsibility.

JH: Can you elaborate on that?

CV: If you count the amount of athletes who have access to me, it comes to about forty people. Now that doesn't sound like too much, but other high performance centres are working with groups of around ten at the most. Some of those centres might have two coaches for those ten athletes so the quality and time they can spend on their athlete's progression is probably a lot more than I can spend. That means I have to ask the athletes to do their own thing and take more responsibility.

JH: Do you consider your athletes good at disciplining themselves, because it must be difficult to keep track of them all?

CV: The athletes tend to be good at going off and training on their own. Whether they are doing the right stuff is another matter. I think someone who comes into our sport is someone who is prepared to act alone; who is self-responsible and self-disciplined, so the problem is not necessarily making them train. The problems are more linked to controlling the athletes when I need to. It's one thing to suggest they might take an easy day, but as soon as they are out of your sight you don't really know whether they are going to run for two hours or bike for four. That's their decision because I cannot operate on a level where I know exactly what every athlete has done every day. I wouldn't mind trying to get to the point where if I suggest to an athlete to do something they will go and do it, for example if I suggest they rest rather than train.

JH: Do you find it difficult to balance athlete empowerment with maintaining control as the coach?

CV: I do, yes, because with athlete empowerment you are trying to give them the option to take responsibility. You almost have to let them make their mistakes, which is not in an 'I told you so' way but you obviously have to explain to them the reasons for whatever has happened and that they actually did have a choice to change the outcome, and what they could have done differently. So it's taking this questioning approach. But I can see now having been in the job for a year where the limitations of that lie; as a coach you need to have a lot of answers, experience and knowledge to do that style of coaching. If you don't then you can get a bit unstuck, because it's difficult to guide an athlete if you don't truly know what's going to happen. It's fine to say, 'Look, I think if you run today you might get ill in the next few days' rather than saying, 'I'm not sure if you should be doing that' and if the athlete asks, 'Why, I feel alright?' you have to have an answer. If you don't have that gut feeling or that strength to say what you think might happen to them, it can be interpreted in a negative way.

JH: We seem to be talking about the performance aspect of the sport but you mentioned that you coach the Student Triathlon Club. Is it difficult for you to coach performance-oriented athletes and participation-oriented athletes?

CV: I think it could get complicated if one of my core values wasn't that I think people need to enjoy themselves. Now you could argue that such a value pushes my coaching slightly towards participation. The trouble with performance and the argument is that elite performers don't need to enjoy themselves. However, I really believe that elite performers do need to enjoy what they are doing otherwise you won't get the best out of them and from what I've seen that seems to be true. So actually, I don't really need to switch between one style and the other. I just make sure that people are doing what they should be doing to make themselves better because, at the end of the day, whether they are participation- or performance-focused, if they are getting better they will be happier. What's tough is that the better an athlete gets the increments of success get smaller. So they have to work harder to be successful. I've been very lucky to work on the participation side with someone who has progressed incredibly quickly over the past year and that's been great and really motivating. On the other hand, I've got an elite performer who has improved a very small amount, but it's trying to make that performer realise that they have improved, where it's not as visible as it used to be.

JH: Do you rely on sport science support to help you with your coaching?

CV: To be honest, I've kept the programme very much under my control.

JH: Why is that?

CV: I think in order for psychologists, nutritionists, strength and conditioning to work well within the programme there has to be a trust between not only the athlete and that person, but also the coach and the external support system. If there's a breakdown of trust in either of those pathways, I don't know if the effectiveness of that person is going to really come through.

JH: Would you say that level of trust is something that comes with time?

CV: Yes, I would. The problem I've got is that I'm trying to develop relationships but it's taking time because although I knew people before hand in the triathlon set up, I knew them as an athlete and not a coach. Now as a coach I think I have to form a slightly different relationship with them. Fortunately, the regime before me had very good relationships, so some of the support services are very happy to work with triathlon. It's basically me knowing what I want that person for, with them trusting me as a fairly novice coach, and me trusting them.

JH: So when you are building these relationships do you think you are predisposed to accept input from the sources you perceive as more reliable? For example, do you feel

pressure from your athletes or other stakeholders to rely on current innovations?

CV: Definitely. Triathletes as people are notoriously keen on gismos, gadgets and kit. Plus we are an endurance-based, physiological sport, and so sports science has always got a journal or an opinion on how to help us get better and quicker. While I appreciate and accept that, I am very keen to keep it more about an athlete's actual ability to perform, rather than what numbers indicate; what they've tested and what that means. My job depends on trying to create someone who's going to stand on an Olympic podium in six or seven years time. Some would argue that I need to know numbers all the time, but I'm not so sure. I think I just need to make sure the athlete gets the best out of themselves on a daily basis, and wants to do their best, so hopefully that way it creates an athlete who automatically goes through those steps to be the best they can be. If they've got the talent they will step on that podium, but if it all gets focused on numbers, and the numbers don't look right, then people get lost.

JH: Do you find it difficult to draw the line between relying on a source of recognised information and compromising your own values?

CV: I think I adapt my philosophy to a certain extent in the current set up that I've got. The performance manager, who is effectively my line manager, is a scientist and therefore there's quite a big emphasis on looking at numbers to determine who's good and who's bad. I do try not to bend my philosophy because of that but try to mould it almost, and say, 'Right, well that works to a certain extent, but I'm not prepared to do that', because, again, I'm still learning and I'm relatively new. I feel like I've got to take on all these different things. So, rather than bending my philosophy I would say it evolves. I don't like to just turn people away flatly, and think what they've got to say is irrelevant and wrong. I do think sport science has a role to play. I just don't know if it's the only role, or if it is the Holy Grail. Coaching is about the ability to give knowledge to an athlete, and, yes, sport science plays a part but it doesn't necessarily mean the athlete has to believe or have everything coming from that aspect.

JH: Do you see the practical application of your philosophy as influential on the way you work and intervene with your athletes?

CV: In theory, yes. I don't think I have formed my philosophy as rigidly as perhaps I need to, but then I would argue from that point that it does take a while for a philosophy to truly form. As I said, I think it's something that evolves; that's the best way to describe it. I've had an example today where I've actually been working with an athlete and three or four months ago I probably wouldn't have trained him, because I believed that recovery was the most important thing. However, for whatever reason, I suddenly ended up trying to help that athlete out by trying to focus more on high-intensity sessions without fully keeping true to my philosophy where recovery is the most important factor. So, there's a prime example of where complications lie. You try to do the best for the athlete, but if you don't have the strength and confidence in your own methods and philosophy, and your philosophy isn't at the forefront of your mind with every decision you make, then I think it's easy to stray from your path.

JH: I'm interested in what you said about your philosophy not being at the forefront of your mind. Do you think the coaching decisions you make come from something more intuitive, rather than actually being something you consciously consider when faced with a situation like this?

CV: For me it's intuitive. Every time I chat to an athlete or try to write a programme for an athlete, I'm actually making a decision based on what I see right there and then. Again, it's a limitation of the coaching set-up I've got here that I don't have enough time to record everything that happens to an athlete, which I actually think does limit some of the decisions I make. I make a decision in a snapshot in time without necessarily considering the history prior to that point, which I think could possibly change what the right course of action is. This is why I like to talk through with an athlete what I think they should do. Because I don't have all of that information there all of the time, I need to get bits of information from them to help them make the right decisions and give them the right advice.

JH: If you had fewer athletes would you consider your job to be a lot easier because you could keep more control and record previous experiences?

CV: I think so. The type of person I am and the style of coaching I try to use I think works on building close personal relationships. They always take time and the person needs to feel that commitment. So if I was to have more time with the athletes and limit the numbers in my squad, I would hope that I could deliver a better service.

JH: You said your coaching philosophy is something that is continually evolving. Do you think you construct it on the basis of what you think is expected of you as a coach or perhaps from your own experiences?

CV: It's forming from both those aspects. It's not just experiential learning, day-to-day activities or speaking with other coaches. It goes back as far as my childhood, when I did sports as a kid and what my parents used to do. They were keen sports people, and I think my upbringing shows through in my coaching. It is everything rolled into one, which is why, without sounding too controversial, I think it's hard to pigeon hole what makes a great coach. A philosophy is built up of everything that has gone on in a person's life and it's why they are always individual, I think, but it's something which, because it evolves, I'm adding to all the time.

JH: Are you saying that rather than being something which is innate, a coach's knowledge is built on their interaction with society?

CV: I think so, yes. As part of a recent coaching qualification I did I was asked to write a coaching philosophy, and then we were asked to re-evaluate that after six weeks or so. I think when I evaluated it I still believed it, but I felt there were other things I could add because I had spoken to 16 other coaches on that course and I had learned from them. The danger comes when you can't decipher information to decide what's useful or not. If you don't come up with good decisions on that information then you're just left with a massive jumble of random information which you can't actually use.

JH: Do you think you decipher the useful and less useful information based on what you think a good coach should be like, so you might act in conformance with what you perceive to be a typical coaching 'persona'?

CV: Yes, I think that definitely comes through. There is this perception that the athlete is expecting a certain thing from you because you're a coach. Fortunately, I became aware of this when I studied, so I try not to let it influence what I do, which I guess sounds like a round-about way of doing it, but I think the way I coach is very much like the way I am. I try not to be two different people: a coach and Chris Volley. I think it's all just one. That way there's some transparency, there's honesty. Now, that means sometimes I fall into the trap of acting the coach, because I might be given a young group of athletes or someone that's new to me, but over time I try to get rid of this acting phase and get back down to the real me or the real them, where we actually understand each other. But, it is difficult in the professional environment because I think there's now an expectation of what a coach does and what a coach should be like. So coming back to your question, yes, I do act sometimes because I don't necessarily have the experience of a long-term coach, but I am aware of it and therefore I always try and be myself when I can.

JH: Do you see that expectation of how you ought to be as having a major role in how you adapt your philosophy?

CV: I think all coaches are very different and it's very hard to classify how a good coach should act. For instance, a swim coach I know never sits down on poolside because that was the performance director's views. He was confident, loud and quite brash with his athletes. Another swim coach I know is very different. He sits on the block by the side of the pool relaxed and will observe and act in a different way. If you ask most people what a coach should act like I think they would say the former one, the one that is brash and loud. And if they had to say which one was the better coach they would probably say the same one. But without accounting for results, I actually prefer the style of the second coach because he's not worried what people think. All he's concerned with is making sure he gives the athlete the right information at the right time, which I don't think you can argue against. I think that's the crux of coaching.

JH: Do you think that because triathlon is an individual sport it influences the relationship you have with your athletes?

CV: I think it does make a difference in an individual sport because each athlete is different and has individual differences which need to be worked on to help them be the best they can be. In a team game I think it's just more management of the group ethos. If you get that right and everyone buys into that it's OK. With individuals it's more difficult, although I think some coaches out there just say, 'This is what the group does, be part of it or don't' and you make your calls based on that. But that's not the way I work or how I want to work with athletes.

JH: Is there much disparity in the way you coach male and female athletes?

CV: I coach them both together. I try not to do anything different between those two groups. We have some incredibly strong women in our squad who are quite useful as tools to motivate some of the guys. It's useful because often the guys don't want to lose to the girls, and it makes the girls feel good to be able to compete with them. The girls perhaps analyse things a little bit more. I don't think I treat people in different ways.

JH: Is that also the case with regard to individual workloads?

CV: I do try to adjust everyone's workloads to suit what they're doing and where they're at, but I still coach the men and women together. I mean, that may not be something which is approved in terms of a sport science perspective, like Istvan Balyi's ideas concerning Long Term Athlete Development, and maybe that's one of the drawbacks of my system.

JH: It appears that in coaching the emphasis is generally on critiquing performers, but how do you go about praising your athletes?

CV: I use praise a lot, probably too much. I'm starting to see, not so much the error of my ways, but the difficulty that can create. As a squad we had a fairly disappointing performance at the weekend at the National Championships and the athletes knew they didn't perform. I know that I didn't necessarily do everything in my power to help them or make them perform, so we were all walking away with our tails between our legs. But I've made sure that we keep it honest and real and just say, 'Right this is what we did wrong, this is what we are going to do to make it right, let's get on with it'. So there is the negative side. I'm setting myself up to say, 'This is what you have got to achieve', so that's where the praise will fall – if you achieve that then you get praise.

JH: How about on a day-to-day basis in training?

CV: On a day-to-day basis I'm happy if an athlete will turn up to a set, do the set to the best of their ability based on what's gone before and what's in the future, so there's a logical decision process being made, and they walk away knowing that they have tried their hardest. That doesn't mean they have worked to exhaustion but that they've done their best training session that day, whether it's an hour easy run, or a 20-minute hard sprint on the track.

JH: Do you believe that an athlete and a coach can learn something from a poor performance?

CV: Yes, certainly. I try to find a positive in everything somebody has done, no matter how bad it appears to be. If something goes wrong then it's really good because you've learned and you've got some knowledge and experience from what's happened, and as long as you take away from it and question why something went wrong, then I think you will improve.

JH: As a society we seem to be fuelled by success in sport. Do you see that shaping the attitudes of your athletes and is that something you have to consider in terms of setting goals?

CV: I think if you only focus on the outcome it's unlikely to ever appear and that's still a phase I'm going through at the moment, where some of the athletes want to see an improvement in their performance and want to be at a different level. I don't really know if many of them actually understand what it's going to take to get to the next level and the process involved. I'm not convinced at the moment that the route that every athlete is taking is necessarily the right route, but until they accept that I can't change anything.

JH: So you think that's something they have to recognise themselves rather than something you can force?

CV: Some coaches would instil it in them, but I think the way I am and the situation I'm in, I've almost got to let them fall before I can pick them up and rebuild them. I'm trying not to let that happen because I hate to see people hurt themselves and fail, but I don't get to the point where I give up on them. I'll just be there, so that if it does go wrong I'm there to help pick up the pieces. Then it's time to give them a shake down as well and say, 'If you want to get there you've got to take these steps'. It's not going to be quick, it's going to take time, effort and hard work, but if they're prepared to do that then we can.

JH: Finally, Chris, is there any advice you would give to coaches who are perhaps starting out, in terms of how they could improve their own practices?

CV: I think it's really just summarising what we've talked about and how you shouldn't feel fixed within your coaching philosophy, knowing that it is constantly evolving and therefore remaining open-minded. Other than that I think it's knowing your own values as a coach and also not being afraid to admit that you don't know everything and that other people's opinions and perspectives can also help you develop.

chapter 9
coach interview:
andy tillson

luke jones

introduction

Association football in the United Kingdom generates global interest and provides entertainment, cultural affiliation and employment for millions. Players at the top of the game are given celebrity status and teams are fanatically supported and analysed both in the public and the media.

Inside this huge, bubble-like environment reside the coaches who strive to achieve success and honours for themselves and their teams. Access to such individuals and the inner circles of football in the United Kingdom is limited. My 'insider' status as a former player, however, has allowed me carry out this in-depth interview with Andy Tillson, a former professional footballer and current head coach of the TeamBath football programme. This interview aims to portray how a coach's experiences contribute to and supplement his own coaching and pedagogical foundations.

Luke Jones: Andy, you are now the head coach at TeamBath FC, can you explain how you came to be in this position?

Andy Tillson: To begin, I have a football background during which I played right through from non-league football and into league football. When I came out of league football I was looking to stay in the game, just like hundreds of players are. I knew about TeamBath and the University of Bath from my time at Bristol Rovers, when we used to train up here [University of Bath] now and again. I wanted to carry on playing, so I came here as a player at the start. Originally I had the intention of seeing how it developed. I wanted to get into coaching, but I didn't think there would be an opportunity here. But once I started playing, we got two promotions and it became apparent that the club was building and becoming bigger and it needed more people to help out. So I started helping with the reserves and became an assistant. It has developed further on from that now with other coaches leaving and I have filled their space.

LJ: You said that many ex-players look to stay in the game. Why do you think this is?

AT: Football is one of those sports you get into and if you love football, then you're going to want to stay within it. Certainly I love the game and there's no better job, being out on the training ground. Also, I think it makes it easier when you finish, because when you finish playing as a player, that's difficult to cope with. The coaching side just helps you to recover from that.

LJ: Did you have a period when you found it difficult after you stopped playing at a high level?

AT: I say to a lot of people that nothing prepares you for that moment: one minute you're a footballer and the next minute you're not. You get very little help with that. You're out in the big bad world on your own.

LJ: Did you ever consider something other than going straight into coaching?

AT: I did. I set up a landscaping business because it was something I did a long time ago and had the qualifications in. But it wasn't the same; I missed football too much.

LJ: You were a captain for Bristol Rovers. Did that help your transition to becoming a coach?

AT: I think it definitely helped being a captain and being presented with the problems that just being a player never really involved. The responsibilities of dealing with things like the media and all the other stuff like organising players. I enjoyed that so much as a captain. I suppose from that point of view it made coaching slightly easier.

LJ: Who provided you with examples of how to coach?

AT: I was lucky to work with some good coaches. I think the best ones were probably the ones that were very organised and the ones where you knew where you stood with. They were very straight and very organised, also they were football people who understood the game. That was a valuable experience.

LJ: Do you think your understanding of the need for a strong support base has made you try to provide that as a coach?

AT: I would like to think so. I think having kids helps as well. It makes you know what people need and you realise the responsibilities involved with looking after other people. That helps, and I'd like to think we try and do our best for our players as people.

LJ: That is important, especially with football being such a results-driven industry. Players can sometimes get a little bit lost if no one is looking after them.

AT: I definitely agree.

LJ: Have you had any experience of that in the past?

AT: Very much so. For example, as a player you are used purely for what you are and there's very little leeway. It's one-way traffic sometimes and you don't get anything back. Some managers have been great at it and other managers have just thought you're there to do a job, so do your job and, if not, then someone else comes in and that's it. But you become a little cynical towards it with time and then you realise that that is part of the game.

LJ: I'd like to move on to your actual approach towards coaching and your coaching philosophy. Do you think that your coaching philosophy has developed as you've become more experienced as a coach?

AT: Definitely. For example, I think there is no god-given right to move from being a player or being a professional player into coaching. I think it was quite difficult, to be honest with you, to start with. It definitely helps the longer you are in it [coaching] and you learn through your own mistakes. You then think more about the game from a coaching perspective. For example, as a player you turn up with your boots on and you know what your job is, but as a coach you have to think about lots of things and you have lots of responsibilities towards your players as well.

LJ: Do you think that it helped being amongst a team of coaches initially instead of being on your own?

AT: I think their experience was a big help and the fact that they had been here a while and gone through what I'd gone through. I think it helps massively in this environment, having people around that can help you and support you.

LJ: What do you think your strengths as a coach are?

AT: I think how I try to draw on my own experiences as a basis to help guide the lads is one of my strengths as a coach. Because I am not so far removed from my days as a player I remember what it's like to be on the other side.

LJ: Do you think that this approach to coaching has developed as a result of working with primarily young players?

AT: Yes, that is true and I'm not saying that it's always right, because I think sometimes being more aggressive can help you with the players. I think that maybe sometimes that's something I need to work on, maybe to be a bit more aggressive at times. As a young player I didn't particularly like it, but I know I've got a few good habits from being hollered and bawled at at times. It's a process of learning, as a developing coach you are learning all the time.

LJ: What do you think makes you different from coaches you've worked with in the past?

AT: I think you're always going to be your own person and you're always going to do things your own way. But I think you do draw on those experiences from other coaches. So, I think you probably find that there is quite a bit of me in other coaches that I've worked with. You will always look at how they would perhaps have dealt with some things as well. I think there is a bit of a mixture really, I don't think I'm particularly unique or a one-off type of coach.

LJ: Do you enjoy learning how to become a better coach?

AT: Definitely. Also, I'm not too sure you ever master coaching, to be honest. I think that as a player it was difficult to master the game and the older you got, the better you became at it. With coaching I think as you become more familiar and more comfortable with different situations, you do get better at it.

LJ: Do you think coaches who have never actually played football professionally have an advantage in some aspects of coaching?

AT: I think sometimes coaches without playing backgrounds are more open-minded, and I think sometimes ex-professionals can be very 'this is the way you're going to do it and that's the way it will be'. And that is because of the culture that they have been used to. Sometimes I think, as well, that players can be put in difficult circumstances; for example, one day you are a player and the next day you are expected to be a good coach. I think that is where somewhere like TeamBath is a great place to learn, because you don't have to go straight into the Football League mentality where it is results driven and where you learn on your feet almost. If you get it wrong in that environment you never get given another chance. I think here you get the chance to learn and the chance to make mistakes and to get better, which is invaluable really.

LJ: Do you think that that has stood you in good stead as you develop as a coach?

AT: Oh definitely, definitely. It really is within a professional environment here. For example, we work with the players every day, the same as at a professional club. So there are very few differences apart from the fact that here you are allowed to learn and to get better without the pressure.

LJ: Do you think that in a way it might be difficult for you to progress further into the professional game, for example, you may be more relaxed and perhaps unprepared for that environment?

AT: I think it will probably help me massively. It would help me, knowing what I know now, the fact that there is a lot to learn. I think that I thought I could step straight into management and coaching when I finished playing, but now I realise that I couldn't have done. Maybe I'm not ready for it yet, but I think that it is definitely the right route for me to go, personally, to get better. Then if opportunities do arise later on, I think that I would be better equipped to take them.

LJ: There has been a lot of talk about coaching badges in the press with Gareth Southgate and Glenn Roeder not possessing the right qualifications. When you were taking your coaching badges how much did they help?

AT: That's a good question. I do realise that you have to do them. I realise you have to get qualified, so there are no short cuts to it. I'm not too sure what you get from them, though. Bits of the courses are very relevant and that helps you with your session planning. I think there is very little interaction and you don't get asked very much about your knowledge of the game. It's just about the way you teach and there's no exam to see how much you know about the game. I think there would be a lot more sense in coach educators being available to talk when you need help. Once you've got your badges and you're qualified you need more support from people like that. Instead of getting your badges and then saying, 'Now you're qualified'. But you're not really! You may have passed a qualification but there's a lot more to learn about the type of sessions. Personally, I think you need constant support.

LJ: Moving on. How healthy do you think it is to get quite close to players? How much do you think you need to keep your distance and maintain an air of authority?

AT: I think different styles exist. At Grimsby we used to train with the manager every day and he used to change in the same dressing room as us and we gained two promotions under him. I think it's just very individual again. Your style of coaching is very much down to whether you have the respect of the players. I think that's important. I think if you lose the respect of your players then you're struggling a little bit. As long as your players respect what you're trying to do for them you're OK.

LJ: When you deliver your coaching sessions, what are the main lessons you want your players to take away? Is it more football development or individual development or just a general rounded development?

AT: I think it will all develop from what happens on a Saturday really. I know we're not concentrating on the result being the be all and end all on a Saturday for us. But we do have to make sure players get better. We also have to concentrate on what the team needs to do to improve, and not knee-jerk reaction stuff. If we've had a real bad spell recently or we are not defending very well, we need to just keep working on it, but I sometimes think sessions need to put on so that the players realise what we are trying to do. I want players to go home and when they are having their tea to think, 'Why did we do that?', and for them to actually realise themselves. I think when we are sitting down and organising our sessions we ensure the players get what they need out of them. It might be a mental thing or a physical thing, or ball related.

LJ: That moves nicely on to discussing the level of power that players should possess in the coach-player relationship. There is a stereotypical view of the coach and manager being above the players, directing and giving orders and things like that. How much do you think players should be involved in the coaching process?

AT: I think it's really good if the players start to realise it's their session and that it's down to them, once the session is put on. I think the older you get as a player the more you realise, 'This isn't a great session' and you know that it's not going well. With experience you say to yourself, 'What can I do to make it work better?'. Players have a responsibility to help the coach if they're struggling to make it work. I think that as a player, every time you step out onto the training ground you need to focus.

Whatever the session is, whether you disagree with it or agree with it, you need to try and get something out of it.

LJ: How do you think you convey that responsibility to the players as a coach?

AT: Well, we do speak about that sort of thing and we do let them know that they need to train the way that they're going to play. That's their responsibility really. I know it's our responsibility to make it enjoyable, make it so they can get something out of it, but their responsibility is to be mentally switched on when they turn up and try and enjoy what they are trying to do.

LJ: How do you think your approach as a coach measures up to the stereotypical view of an autocratic leader?

AT: Again, I think the way I act depends on how we play on a Saturday. I think that's the measure of how the training sessions are going. If every time you go onto the training ground you think, 'That was terrible', and if we are playing poorly on a Saturday, I think you really have to look at yourself and think 'Why are we not training very well and not playing very well?' Obviously, if it happens regularly, it's not the players' fault, we do look at ourselves and consider how much or how little we are in control. Regular self-assessment is key.

LJ: In a lot of football clubs within the UK there is a big differ-ence between being a football coach and a manager. A lot of the time a coach works underneath the manager. That is also the position you find yourself in at Bath. How is your coaching approach affected by having someone that you essentially work under?

AT: As a coach you need to have a good relationship with the manager. That's vital. You need to know exactly what he wants out of the sessions. Also, if the manager is not able to get out there, you need to make sure that what he wants out of the sessions gets done. I think it's fine, but it's better when the manager coaches as well. I don't think there is a place for just being the manager and sitting in the office any more. I think that's kind of old school.

LJ: Do you think that across the game this approach is fading away?

AT: Yes, and I think that it's right, too. I think that as a manager you need some sort of level of input and to get out there and get your point across.

LJ: Do you ever feel restricted as a coach, working directly underneath a manager?

AT: Not really, I don't see it that way. I mean, being honest with you, I think as long as you have good contact with the manager that's what is important. I think that if you don't have good contact with your manager it becomes difficult, but as long as you have a good working relationship then it can be really good. I've never experienced any major problems with that.

LJ: I'd now like to talk about the level of resources available to you as a coach and how that affects the way you approach coaching. Do you think the fact that you have a lot of good resources at your disposal here has helped you?

AT: I think it has definitely helped us. We go out onto good training pitches everyday and automatically that helps players. If you put them on a terrible pitch then they start to think, 'I'm not enjoying this'. Access to good facilities and equipment, we have lots of that around the place, and more than football-based stuff like swimming pools and hydrotherapy pools. I think it's important to use all those things as well.

LJ: How do you deal with the varying ability of the players underneath you? You have been here for a while and every season you have had a different bunch of players with differing levels of abilities. How have you managed to adapt as a coach? For example, dealing with players of less ability and more heart, or vice versa?

AT: I think that's definitely something that we speak to a lot of coaches about, how you can improve as a club, and it all comes down to recruitment really. Recruiting the players, because better players will always get you a better standard of club and football, I suppose. Personally, a good attitude is also great for me. If someone lacks that little bit of ability but has a great attitude I think the coaches will work with them all day. There is a lot to be said for getting a fine balance between talent and attitude.

LJ: You have talked about having a good attitude, what sort of things do you think that entails?

AT: I think self-discipline really. We regularly come out with the ingredients of being a good footballer, which include consistency of performance and aggression. Also you have to have the ability to analyse yourself as a player. If a player has a good attitude then he usually has four or five of those key components.

LJ: How much, then, do you think the coach can initiate those attributes or how much is the responsibility of the players?

AT: I think the responsibility is with the coach. I think the coach can get 10–20 per cent more out of a player on each one of those attributes. But essentially the player has a bigger responsibility.

Also, when someone has poor discipline it's very easy to 'bin' them, but as a coach you need to improve their discipline, and if it's ability then you need to try and develop their ability. It's a wide range of things coaches do to maximise their players' potential.

LJ: Turning to a different subject, considering your time playing in a professional environment and also now at TeamBath, I'd like to talk about the pressure put on players and how as a coach you can deal with that. Although TeamBath don't play in the professional league, it is still a high-performance environment. How do you think that as a coach you deal with this pressure?

AT: I think that's another really good question. It's important to consider and we have sat and analysed this a lot recently. Do we put too much pressure on people? The answer that I keep coming up with is probably that we do need to. Coming from the professional environment where you don't suffer fools lightly, you have to do your job. If you don't, lots of people lose out, and if you want to stay in that job for a long time, then that's the sort of attitude you need. But it is different being a coach. It's also different being here with young players trying to learn the game. More often I'm trying to back away from that and to take a little bit of pressure off the lads. It has taken me a while to consider that 'maybe this is something we need to look at' to foster their development as players and not assume they know everything.

list of contributors

Zoe Avner is currently a postgraduate student in Education/ Coaching at the University of Bath, England. This follows her honours undergraduate studies at the Sorbonne, Paris and Rutgers University in the US. Her research interests stem from her personal experience as a female football player in different cultural settings. She has played high level female football at the club level in France, Canada, the US and England and represented the French national team at under 19 and under 21 levels. She is interested in how sports are 'gendered' and socially constructed. She is also interested in investigating how identities are constructed and negotiated within high-level sports. She has coached both in the US and in Canada and would like to work for an organisation that helps to develop sport in developing countries.

Eric Anderson is a Lecturer in the Department of Education at the University of Bath, England. He uses qualitative methods to investigate the construction of masculinity and sexuality among university-aged men. His most recent book, *In the Game: Gay Athletes and the Cult of Masculinity* (2005), examines the construction of masculinity in the sport setting and how openly gay athletes navigate and challenge this institution. Anderson is also an accomplished running coach having worked with athletes of all ages and abilities in the US and England.

Iain Bates is a Performance Tennis Coach at the University of Bath, England, and is responsible for coaching a range of players including five of Britain's top junior prospects. He has also led the British National Junior Team to major events around the world including the European Individual and Team Championships and the Junior Orange Bowl in Florida. A University of Bath graduate in Coach Education, he has a research interest in coaching knowledge and the factors which influence its construction. He co-authored a paper titled 'The making of an expert coach: The construction of coaching knowledge' (Bates & Jones, 2005), which was presented at the Exercise Science, Sports Medicine and Sports Psychology Symposium at Cardiff University, Wales in 2005.

Imornefe Bowes is a Teaching Fellow in the Department of Sports Development and Recreation at the University of Bath, England, where he lectures in coach education and sports psychology. Currently a PhD candidate at the University of Wales Institute Cardiff, his primary research interest is the nature of coach–athlete interactions. As head coach of the University of Bath's high-performance volleyball programme, and a former senior international player he has a vested interest in the application of theoretical knowledge. Through collaborations with supervisor Robyn L. Jones he is examining the application complexity theory to better understand sports coaching.

Anthony Bush is a lecturer in Sports Studies, Education and Coaching, in the Department of Education at the University of Bath, England. Reconceptualising the act of coaching is central to the work of Bush who, by challenging the limitations of current research approaches, is developing a theoretical perspective which understands coaching as a complex, dynamic, social process. Bush draws upon knowledge acquired through his 20 years of active coaching, 10 years as a professional badminton player, and his experiences as a qualified physical education teacher.

Jim Denison is an Associate Professor in the Faculty of Physical Education and Recreation, University of Alberta, Canada. His research concerns how athletes' and coaches' identities are lived into existence and experienced. He co-edited, *Moving Writing: Crafting Movement in Sport Research* (2003, Peter Lang), a scholarly monograph outlining various ethnographic writing practices in sport studies, and wrote *Bannister and Beyond: The Mystique of the Four-Minute Mile* (2004, Breakaway Books) and *The Greatest* (2004, Breakaway Books), the authorised biography of Haile Gebrselassie. Denison is also active as a middle-distance running coach and highly involved in coach education through the Canadian Athletics Coaching Centre.

Jennifer Hardes graduated from the University of Bath, England in Coach Education and Sports Development. In her final year she received the British Olympic Foundation's award for academic excellence. Currently she is pursuing a Masters degree in Sport and Exercise Humanities at the Ohio State University, US. Her research interests are in critical theory, sport philosophy, cultural studies and ethics. Hardes has coaching experience in field hockey and currently holds an appointment as a Graduate Teaching Associate in the Sports Fitness and Health Program at Ohio State.

Luke Jones earned a Masters degree in Sports Coaching from the University of Bath, England, in 2006. His research incorporates the narrative approach to portray the various lived experiences of soccer players in the UK including the effect of injury upon athletic identity. A former Youth International and semi-professional soccer player, Jones has a keen interest in athlete development.

Pirkko Markula is a Professor in the Faculty of Physical Education and Recreation, University of Alberta, Canada. Her research focuses primarily on women's experiences within sport, fitness and physical activity. She edited *Feminist Sport Studies: Sharing Joy, Sharing Pain* (2005, SUNY Press), co-edited *Moving Writing: Crafting Movement in Sport Research* (2003, Peter Lang) and co-authored *Foucault, Sport and Exercise: Power, Knowledge and Transforming the Self* (Routledge, 2006).

Montserrat Martin is a Lecturer in Sociology of Sport and is currently with the Department of Science and Social Sciences at the University of Vic, Barcelona. Her research interests include sexual difference theory and issues related to gender and team contact sports, with a particular focus on rugby.

Leanne Norman is a final year PhD student and teaching fellow within the Department of Education at the University of Bath, England. Her research interests include gender and sport, specifically sport feminism and the empowerment of women coaches and leaders to reach powerful positions in the organisation of sport. Norman also has extensive experience as both a soccer and field hockey coach as well as still being an active player.

index

ableism 32–3, 37–8
active listening 89
augmented feedback 91–2

coach-athlete relationships 29–30, 51, 53–6, 60–1, 211–12
    youth sport 68–77, 79
coach-manager relationships 213–14
coach-parent relationships 68–77, 79
coaches
    ethical goals 79–80
    female 161–81
    identity, formation of 40–3
    qualifications 209–10
    and social exclusion 36–43
    structural/cultural influences on 43–5
    transition to, for athletes 183–200, 202–4
coaching
    alternative strategies 121, 126–7, 128–30
    approaches to 8–12, 58–9
    for elite young athletes 130–4
    expansion as academic discipline 3–5
    and experiential learning theory 125–7
    science/art debate 6–8
    structured reflection 127–8
coaching philosophies 118–19, 190–6, 205
coaching styles 57–8, 66–7, 175
cognitive psychology 97
communication 85–109
    constructivist approach 94–5
    evaluation 107–8
    feedback and 90–3
    instruction 92
    model of 87–9
    non-verbal 88–9, 103–4
    perception and 102–5
    performance profiles 106–7
    process of 87–8
    schema theory 96–105
    subtext 93–7
    uses of 90–105
    verbal 90–3
    video-stimulated recall 105–6
continuous professional development (CPD) 138
credible coaching 56–7
culture of sport 28

discourses (Foucault) 146, 157–8
disengagement effect 42

early identity foreclosure 154
experience, and performance 115–18, 144
experiential learning theory 114, 117–24
    alternative strategies 120–2, 128–30
    and coaching 125–7
    evaluation 122
    reflection in 119–26
    structured reflection 127–8

feedback 90–3

gender issues 138–58, 161–81, 197
    misogyny 30–1, 36, 165–6
    sexual politics 61–8, 78–9
    sexual violence 31
    stereotyping 178–9

homophobia 31–2, 36, 174
hybridity/diversity strategy 155–6

identity 40–3, 140, 146, 151–2, 154, 156

inclusive coaching strategies 45–7
inclusivity/exclusivity 25–6
instantiation 99–100
inter-subjectivity 95
International Paralympic Committee (IPC) 33

knowledge, creation of 16, 86, 89, 118
knowledge of performance (KP) 91
knowledge of results (KR) 91

listening 89

memory 99–100
mental toughness 139, 143
    models of 147–9, 152–4
    psychological research on 152–7

Nominal Group Technique (NGT) 108
non-verbal communication 88–9, 103–4

Olympic Games, London 2012: 5–6
organisational socialisation 141

Paralympics 5, 33
perception 102–5
performance, and experience 115–18, 144
performance profiles 106–7
power
    in coach-athlete relationships 53–6, 60–1, 211–12
    ethical use of 55–6
    types of 28–30
professionalism 145–6

racism 33–5, 38–9
reflection 127–9
    and CPD 135
    in experiential learning theory 119–26
    structured 127–8
respect 15, 44, 51–80, 210
    in coach-athlete relationships 29–30, 54–5, 60–1, 184–5
    ethics of 53–77

schema theory 96–105
    bottom-up (data-driven) activation 102
    cognitive psychology 97
    communication and 96–105
    default values 98, 100–1
    instantiation 99–100
    memory 99–101
    non-verbal communication and 103–4
    perception and 102–5
    prototypes 98, 100
    stereotypes 98–9, 104
    top-down (conceptually driven) activation 101
    variable constraints 98
self, see identity
self-esteem 25
self-perception 105
social cohesion/division 25
social exclusion, coaches and 36–43
social structure of sport 26–7
stereotypes 98–9
structured reflection 127–8

verbal feedback 91
video analysis 129–30
video-stimulated recall 105–6
violence 35–6, 39
    sexual 31